IMAGINARY ORIGINS:
SELECTED POEMS

ACKNOWLEDGEMENTS

Appreciation is expressed to the editors of the following magazines in which some of these poems originally appeared: *Antigonish Review*, *Arc*, *ARIEL*, *Bywords*, *Canadian Forum*, *Canadian Literature*, *Canadian Ethnic Studies*, *Chandrabhaga* (India), *Contemporary Verse II*, *Critical Quarterly* (UK), *Cross-Canada Writers' Quarterly*, *Dandelion*, *Fiddlehead*, *Kunapipi* (Denmark/Australia), *Laomedon Review*, *Poetry Canada Review*, *Prism International*, *Quarry*, *Sweven*, *Sandesh*, *This Magazine*, *The Toronto South Asian Review* (now *Toronto International Review*), *Valpariso Review*, *electronic* (USA), *Wasafiri* (UK), *Waves*, *Whetstone*, and *World Literature Today* (USA).

Some of these poems also appeared in: *A Concert of Voices: An Anthology of World Writing in English* (Broadview Press); *A Shapely Fire: Changing the Literary Landscape* (Mosaic Press); *Another Way to Dance: Contemporary Asian Poetry in Canada and the US* (TSAR Publications); *Arrivals: Canadian Poetry in the Eighties* (Greenfield Review Press, New York); *Breaking Silence: An Anthology of Asian-American Poetry* (Greenfield Review); *Canada: Native Peoples and Immigrants* (Myrdal Press, Denmark); *Canadian Voices* (Pencraft International, India); *Companeros: An Anthology of Writings About Latin America* (Cormorant Books); *Crossing the Water* (Greenfield Review Press); *Heinemann Book of Caribbean Poetry* (UK); *They Came in Ships* (Peepal Tree Press, UK); *India in the Caribbean* (Hansib Publishing, UK); *Jahagi Bhai* (TSAR); *Making a Difference: Canadian Multicultural Literature* (Oxford University Press); *Ottawa: A Literary Portrait* (Pottersfield Press); *Parthenon Poetry Anthology* (New York); *Penguin Book of Caribbean Verse* (UK); *Presence de L'Inde dans le Monde* (Edition L'Harmattan, Paris); *Six Ottawa Poets* (Mosaic Press); *The Geography of Silence* (TSAR); and *This is My Best* (Coach House Press).

I thank the Canada Council, the Ontario Arts Council, and the City of Ottawa for small grants over the years to keep me engaged in this ongoing process.

IMAGINARY ORIGINS:
SELECTED POEMS
1977-2002

CYRIL DABYDEEN

PEEPAL TREE

First published in Great Britain in 2004
Reprinted in 2012
Peepal Tree Press Ltd
17 King's Avenue
Leeds LS6 1QS
UK

ISBN 9781900715942

Supported using public funding by
ARTS COUNCIL
ENGLAND

CONTENTS

INTRODUCTION

The poems in this collection are drawn from books published between 1977 and 1997 and more recent uncollected poems. They are poems which were mostly written since my arrival in Canada in 1970. Poems written in the 1960s, when I started writing in Guyana, have not been collected here. Most are lost and I've begun to view what's left of them as work from my "beginning" period of writing. Nevertheless, in these early poems I believe I began exploring some of the themes developed in subsequent collections. At the core of these themes is an engagement with memory (indeed an importunate sense of origins), coupled with reflections on a changing self as it responds to Caribbean as well as Canadian temperaments and landscapes as they are internalised within me. I sense, though, that within the changing self there are some more continuous promptings. These are explored in my poems as a deep attraction to what I can best describe as a 'hinterland spirit'. And though poems speak of loss and dislocation, I think I have found my truest poetic self in the crossing of boundaries, and the necessity of looking in different directions. Not unexpectedly, in this collection there are poems reflecting the confessional and the mythopoeic – as well as the realistic – as I combine my diasporic and immigrant selves. This sense of being Janus-faced will no doubt continue to dictate how I write.

Beyond this, my sense of having been born with Guyanese and Caribbean sensibilities – and now living in Canada for most of my adult life – has instilled in me the value of forming ties that embrace the so-called New World, ties of history, politics, and cultural sharing. And because of my Asian roots and ancestry, and European traditions always at work, I have formed both an insider and outsider perspective on what I keep confronting – all reflected in immediate and personal ways in my poems.

The intention here is to give the reader not only a broad range, but to follow the threads of what has developed in me over the years. I have not always included what I consider some of my best poems for this collection: for instance, from *Discussing Columbus* (1997), I have not chosen the long poem "Caribbees," first drafted in 1975. My overriding principle in *Imaginary Origins* has been to put together a retrospective collection that traces the flux of time and change as I've come to grips with my feelings while straddling past and present, and aimed to discover who I am.

Indeed, these poems bring home to me the sense of a wilful act in exploring my growth towards being a writer – if perhaps only a post-colonial one – all the while recording my responses to the diverse experiences, peoples, and emotions I daily encounter. Other readers with a more detached eye and ear might disagree with my choices in this collection. I won't argue with that, albeit there are choices I have made from gauging the responses I've received over the years in my readings across Canada, the US, UK and Europe, Asia and the Caribbean.

Each poem in this volume, I feel, is akin to a "moment's monument," and no doubt, even as "occasional" poems – as some appear to be – they stand on their own as I try to maintain integrity and simultaneously hone my craft as a writer. Suffice it to say, I aim to form ties with my deepest instincts as I fashion new work, drawing on the feeling of having a heterogenous, or even a hybrid consciousness as an artist, though one perhaps always responding to the spirit of place, if sometimes only in imaginary ways. New experiences continue to be transmuted into poems by a "shaping of connections" (W.H. New) through the alchemy of the spirit.

I've lived now in Ottawa for over twenty-five years (and elsewhere in Canada) and spent the first three seminal years in the Lakehead, or Lake Superior region – not unlike Margaret Atwood herself, who described her own experience there as "an excellent place to spend your formative years." This early experience contributed to my initial grounding in Canadian literature, with a concomitant sense of the immediacy of the Great White North always inspiring beauty and awe, though also bringing home to me the immediate survival instincts of "a drawer of water and hewer of wood" – my own pioneering days, if only as a tree-planter, and living with Native peoples in forest camps in that region.

In that period I first met the late sound poet, bp nichol, and became acquainted with the works of Isabella Valency Crawford, E.J. Pratt, A.M. Klein, Earle Birney and others. Later in Ottawa I discovered more fully the poetry of the likes of D.C. Scott and Bliss Carman; and when I became a member of the League of Canadian Poets got to know F. R. Scott, Miriam Waddington, P.K. Page and others. All these impacted on my Caribbean consciousness and sensibility and enabled me to broaden the tradition I write from.

The urge to hone my skills as a writer will keep pushing me to extend my connections to the wider community of like-minded souls. I continue to benefit from sharing insights with others, including family and friends, especially those writers close to home, like Ottawa poet Seymour Mayne, whose advice I've always cherished, or Joy Kogawa – who lived in Ottawa around the time when I first conceived the ideas for some of these poems; and to others like novelist M.G. Vassanji in Toronto, and in the UK the scholar and publisher Jeremy Poynting whose encouragement I shall always be grateful for.

All the while I keep being conscious of the changing possibilities inherent in the creative imagination acting in us, and with us, always. Above all, it is my instinct that there is an elixir of the human spirit, and my search for it, which encourages me to go beyond mundane experience in exploring the complex tapestry of how we live as humans.

Cyril Dabydeen
December 31, 2002

from

GOATSONG (1977)

TAURUS

The wild bull's
on his way. I do
not give myself
too easily.
The lasso-man
enters the scene
trying to grapple
with horns.

My father hammers
at the portals
of his mistress's
womb; the bull
bellows across
the fraudulent
road.

My mother spins
her sewing machine
like a solitary
queen. I merely
join with
the spinning.

ABSENCES

Dull absences, then another letter
– Mother, so long –
tells about the unfaithful husband
you married, who never married you,
how you pedalled and pined, for how long?

The village and the town merged.
Bread-seller, there's yeasty emotion
in the bargain. Only love does not rise.
You succumbed to his proposition.
You sold yourself in the making.

A tug at the womb – new life.
The children like loaves came one by one.
So many times over you nearly died
without knowing that you were best –
stitching time, each needle step

an egg. So waiting for nine months
for this – it came at last!
He does not know. I imagine him drinking
himself to oblivion in the oven-like heat –
still talking loudest!

TRAIL

In the lassoing
cow domain nothing
new happens from
the beginning
to the end
of each year
save for the cornucopia
in the wild bush
where roses erupt
bloodlike.

And my father who was
lost in the forest
for forty days
gorged on wild berries
until the lassoing
men converged on
his trail
and eventually found
him half-dead.

I was not born then
before the agony
of the bull
and the dismembered
horns in tropical
south america.

VIRTUE OUT OF NECESSITY

In dog country they
still go to church.

Watch them snarl
before the altar,

yap at the offering
plate. Entering,

he talks of the man
who rode upon his ass

of air. I return home
like a prodigal.

I see my father starving,
his children's

undernourished bodies
anointed by the canine sun.

VIRGINS & REFORMERS

At twenty-two
still a virgin.
You are taken
to a brothel on Pitt
Street, Abraham
van Pere's town.
You try to reform
your first whore.
Above the rickety
building, a glimmer:
moonface.

Give him a false name.
Tell him your parents
wanted you to leave home.
Your second girl.
You tell her the story
of your first love:
how the moon turned pale.
Listen, Tolstoy was
too old. Grey beards
will not reform
the world.

LETTER

You have not written
these past weeks:
a mail strike perhaps.

I do not give up
easily: remembering
old words

like salted cod
in the penury of taste,
and the dim slaves

with their leather
tongues; the indentured
also grew accustomed

to neglect
in the humid heat.
Oh your historic mind –

the words do not
come to remind me
of that country

where they eat men.

MEETING

for Kate

I have dated this girl
from Bombay. She says
she's a Parsee; she doesn't
blink an eye.

The Punjabi who has sheared
his long hair and no longer
wears a turban, who has since
been to Liverpool and Dublin

says I am hundred years
behind: the indentured
system has separated us.

I turn to the Parsee
who tells me about hovering
vultures in Bombay.

Read any Indian novel:
always vultures hovering
above that city.

I long to take her in my arms.
I imagine the Tower of Silence.
The Punjabi looks at me
with a quizzical eye.

THERE'S NO COW

There's no cow
like a Hindu's cow
upon green grass fed
this cow a gentle cow
will not die
will not reincarnate
instead
such sacredness
surrounds this cow
weighed down
with amiableness
she has no need
for bells this cow
no sex will she have
an aureole cow
on a whom a mantra's
said
such boredom felt
until one day when
suddenly chased
by a horned bull
she went on a
rampage
crushing hibiscus
colouring the streets
red
this cow
quickly loses
her blessedness.

PATIENT & OTHERS

I can tell this story
again and again
of gaping wrists,
how you're always
wanting to know,
and I can only lie
about the damned
accidents
          taking place

More than three
years since,
remembering how
she drank the pills,
and the body shaking,
stomach rebelling;
memory dimmed
after shock treatment

No one else knowing
in the same ward,
and we separate
to go on our different
worlds   she wanting
to travel from city
to city, as if
we're always
meant to be
          apart

GROSSE ILE

They perished
forty thousand
from across
the sea —
all immigrants
trying to start
a new life. Typhus raged.
        They died.
        Forty thousand
        skeletons were
        found here
        where a quarantine
        station now stands.
Someone's
        searching for a documentary
        to stir up
        the ghost of
        the living.

LADY ICARUS

"ordered deported – for the fifth time."

You fell, you
fell from seven
stories high
tempting gravity
from the Stratchona
Hotel

not skyward
only landward

like a recalcitrant
angel, Maria,
all the way
        from Ecuador

you came, wanting
desperately to stay
in Canada

        so glorious
and free – defying
another deportation
order when suddenly
your rope

of sheets and blankets
        broke
no sun now melting wax
your hold snaps

        as you plunge
to sudden death
we stand on guard for thee
oh so glorious and free

O Canada O Canada

SEÑORITA

This Señorita from the Dominican
Republic flashes a smile;
she tells me she had attended school
in Canada, is interested in Lope de Vega
and extols the Golden Age of Spain.

I remind her of Pablo Neruda
and Nicolas Guillen,
both closer to her home.
She still smiles, professes
a dim acquaintance with the poetry

of both, talks about water imagery
in Neruda. I remind her about the latter's
fire of love, the Cuban's revolutionary
zeal. She's not impressed;
she still smiles, however.

How about the poets
of the Dominican Republic?
She smiles once more, "Ah, do you
not see I have been educated
in Canada?" she protests innocently.

"Five million people there –
surely there must be poets!"
I exclaim in silent rage.
Once more the Señorita smiles –
bewitching as a metaphor.

GOATSONG

Only goatsong, mind you,
I sing, sing of brother
tramping the lanes
where the dogs are snarling
while with goatsong
we howl, bleat with the sheep,
neigh with the horse
and cackle in the fowls'
barnyard commotion.

I'm no owner of a gun
to scatter the danger
of the squawking night
when goatsong is about,
an aunt drunk as daylight
downing the bootleg rum
upon the throat of the yard.

I sing, I sing now
of the howl and the screech
and the lice in the hair
of a niece crying
with her broom
in the swelling tide
of the dark.

NEPHEW

Alone in the street
this five-year old
wanders, his belly
hanging out like a placard.
The village women
do not notice his slogan;
they merely laugh.
Watching him
I am convinced
he's nothing more
than a fanatic.

GREEN LAND

green is green
in a forest
nondescript
as coconuts

browned in the sun
ablaze with the eyes
of a baboon

and monkeys black
as rain-clouds
as coffee-coloured
creek water

with the torch-lit eyes
of alligators
that cough like a child

in an emerald night

TENANTS

Dog-days downtown
sneering Queen St.
after Princess

feline and rabbit-struck –
how the loyal lady
talks of an old stove

urging disaster.
In the cellar, a dachshund-
huge rat serves no

master or mistress;
he only wreaks royal
havoc in spite of a loaf

of bread each day,
knocking without protocol,
breaking wood and plaster

for the sake of wheat
in the cold and damp
while children huddle

together
in the absence
of a father.

HISTORY

I could remember
you climbing
down from the sun
and standing there
watching –
your eyes made
of steel
swords your teeth
metal your skin

Oh, the gods have
let us down
     We are filled
with centuries
     of awe
Where can we run now?
I only succumb
paving the city streets
     gold to quench
your longing
     for the yellow dust
I am the flower
lop me off
     enter the
darkening time
your clanging march
     bruising us
more than a sacrifice
     I bleed
to an untimely death
     & the gods
are to blame –

Sun's fiercest

ANTHEM

Words fall like
blocks of wood
we remember them
godforsaken
cliches that are
no blessings
to the mouth
your parched lips
quivering tongue
it were better
if you were dumb
  then
    today
hewn to the pith
you become the axe-
man aware of the
tribe's dialect
  remember
    there's
glory in the universe
  of words
Father
  forgive the wooden
    tongue.

from

DISTANCES (1977)

POET SPEAKS TO THE HOUSE

The poet speaks to the house on fire;
the house speaks back

with tongues licking out.
The poet answers with a hand

chopping air, voice raised louder.
Other houses listen to the conversation:

they will remember the dialogue
between words and sawdust, words

and flame, words and trees,
etchings on the memory –

all voices, all words, tongues of fire –
until a man hacked his way

through a door to make
a solid entry.

AFTER THE RAIN

Things will grow
roots needling down
into the humid
evergreen world

(one's roots are
there/will always
be there despite
the constant blurring
taking place
over time)

though small
they'll loosen
up the soil
      such peculiar
      things during
      the night
          all tubular
          like worms.

We watch from this
distance how
they shoot out
like miracles
      such silent stars
      in our famished
lives
      Next day
more seed
more joy
on this soggy
face of earth.

THE FAT MEN

I.

The porch diminishes the fat men.
The fat men diminish the porch.
They play a game with their broad tongues.
The wind rattles the roof, and a house
comes down with the thunderclap
of wild laughter.

No one will tame them, these men
of the earth: these players who sit still,
their bellies growing huge as houses.
One is a cloud, with the sun coming
between his eyes.

II.

Maupassant would have found use
for these men: their spacious under-arms
as incubators – chickens like apples
rolling out from the sun of their armpits –
the organic heat of body, the sweat
of sun, the rattling of board bodies,
the sun and the rain.

III.

The soil knows no difference.
Not only the French have their fat men.
They are the productive of the earth.

*IMAGINARY ORIGINS

From among cows
you blossom,
out of offal
pungent in the air.
You throw a lasso
and grapple
with horns.

A bull's bleached
skull is monument
on a rotten fence:
good luck's in the air.
The season of rum
triumphs in a calf's
high-pitched cry.

There's a fire
smouldering
and prongs
are alive this
minute: alive
with the life
and burnt skin.

*Originally appeared as "Maestro"

FRUIT,

of the earth

I imagine myself
a mouth

you an apple
me a mother-mouth
brother-mouth
sister-mouth
munching, munching

remembering how
once upon a time
the season was
palpable escape
with the slice
white slice/red slice

eagerly munching
aunt-mouth
grandmother-mouth
before balance of
payments became crucial
in a tropical state

when suddenly
star-apple, mango
papaw, sapodilla
take their place
oozing a nation's
sweet distaste.

RATCATCHER

I open the dead body.
Your arm comes
out in the shape of
a rathead. I am calm.
The trap is in my hand.
We clasp. Today we
give the universe
a body. The old cat is
silent in its corner
under a table. Stubborn
as always, it comes to
me like a prodigal.

Where is your rathead?
I am the catcher; I
need another trap with
solid jaws
more solid than
yours. The leaves
are folding. Wet fur.
Born as decaying
leaves. Soggy as a rathead.
The shining steel of
the trap is in your
hand. Your universe
of fleet-footed fur.

CITY

Only the sounds,
city-made

the quiet punctured
holes, holes
our openings

the perforated hour.
No stopping
of orifices

from garden to
limestone city.

Sisters-in-law
their elegance
shaped senses
to perfection.

I do not linger
too long among
hibiscus, bougainvillea.
Sun blossoms

radiance.
I take this
corolla for keepsake.

Flame flowers merely
replace nose, ears, mouth.

Seconds auger day.

THIS IS IT

The tame life:
the animals here
do not look at you –
they converge,
converge.

Thousands
of miles away
it's the same
nightmare: a leviathan
in a water-laced

dream. Entering
once more, huddling
against the cold
in northwestern
ontario

we notice that footprints
are here too,
our mild reckoning
from country
to country.

from

THIS PLANET EARTH (1979)

OFFSPRINGS

I am far away. Meanwhile
sisters and nieces
have ways of getting fat.
I return home after three years.
I notice a few strange
ones around, holding on
to frocks, skirts.
I take them up in my arms.
Mothers remind them never to forget.
Always remember him.
Some storehouse of affection perhaps.
They do not understand.
I will return again
after another three years
expecting more strange faces.
I take a few pictures this time.
Occasionally will look at them.
Show friends once in a while.
Alone now, I mull over events,
thinking, with what expression
shall they greet me, how shall
      I perform next?

SLEUTHING
for David and Judy

Not yet the full
dead of night –

we're not body-hunters
scavengers –

being here merely
to pay homage

to link spirit
with the founding father

Sir John A Macdonald
searching among gravestones

for an epitaph that will tell
in more than words

that he lived here
died in Kingston

city of lore and poverty
north side south side

ramshackle time
bringing us closer together

in the ghost of a haunting.

CANADA DAY

Going over the world
our modern cartographers

in Vespucci haste
some new world lingerers –

no longer in old sow Europe
in another city now –

on vacation
getting wet in the rain

on Parliament Hill, Canada Day,
forsaking sun

and sea
(and you say Danish women only
sing when they're drunk)

watching you towelling
your thighs – your thighs

another world hastily mapped –
instant cartography

COMMOTION

Entering the wildside
of your tropical world

a splashing river night
amid the crackle

of blackened leaves
metallic whirr of insects

I journey through bush
a winding alligator creek

clinging to bamboo posts
and banana leaves

in a makeshift world
I am Raleigh hacking

my way through an Arawak trail
deeper into the heartland

I ply with canoe, casting
in the darkness with eyes

wide open, waiting for the leviathan's
commotion to render a coastland

into solid fragments of memory.

VILLAGE

The village is a sprawled waste
where an old woman with gnarled hands
sweeps the floor under the house

Her grandson squints at the sun
collecting cobwebs from the remnants
of her ramshackle heart

Here the vagrants daily conspire
to capture the moon and hold her ransom
to beckon the sun into oblivion

& the old woman sensing this
mutters a warning – fearing
the fate of the incorrigible young

She wonders about him collecting
jewels for his dungheap
outshining the stars
setting his heart ablaze

& she dreams of a darkening
time when they will both
be watching the fugitives
on the run

WHEN THEY CAME

When they came
they rode trucks
along the main
road of my youth

they held bayonets
stiffly against
their faces
tongues sticking out
like barbed wire

we dared not look
for long
we lived on
in the nightmare
thinking we couldn't
govern a country

we couldn't hold
our own
until the troops came –
men laughing hyena-like
blocking the roads
with eyes of steel
lips ribbed in metal

I watch from
this distance
nurturing fables
one after another

all fragments
of a life

BRAZIL

I have watched Brazil
on the screen like a wound
that needs dressing

I dislike Copacabana for its
waves that do not lash

I watch the boy with one eye gone
hoping that he will appear
like Orpheus

with his guitar to take
the sun
by surprise

In the meantime, I understand
the shame of the outhouse
without doors

the bathroom
without cover

and I am confused in Canada
because I can hardly shake a fist
at the wind. I am too tame.

Sun, do not rob me of this anger.

SEEKING LIGHT

I refuse to burrow, cave-world, underground
domain, this time without light.

I imagine I'd need less heat,
more protection from those who follow

from behind. I burrow still;
I am worm, I am weasel and beaver.

I hold the ground at the tip of my lips,
at the corridor of nose and ear.

I listen to the secrets of the soil;
I talk to the particles of dust in the clear air

amidst the shadow of an overloaded forehead,
hair knotted, gnarled hands digging

for sun. I venture out, I am free amidst
this space, dancing in the claustrophobia

of light. Here the world begins and empties
itself out. My face protrudes with the elemental

mask. Where am I?
What do I listen to next?

TAKING HER HOME

He walks about in the nude before
his children, imagining a rose
in his lapel; his daughter in my arms
now doesn't want to be called darling –

it's too much like a father-and-mother
game. She grew up without guilt;
I look at the clothes in her eyebrows;
she mine, as we touch in palpable light.

Tomorrow, she says, we must protest
against the cobalt bomb
at the American Embassy.
With clothes on we dance

before the crowd of onlookers.
Smoke rises, as her parents
appear with leaves around their waists –

an Adam-and-Eve beginning.
Now with wild embraces,
snarls and shouts,
protests from every side.

Without words, we walk around
in a circle, caring for one another.
Despite love we still burn.

LESBIANS

They do things
to themselves

they do they do
mutters an old man

watching two women
in their twenties

naked – lounging
in the corridor

parading their
lesbianism (it seems)

Affronted
he hurries to the Basilica

praying before an image
of the Virgin Mary

That night he dreams
of an anointing

the women's bodies
supple and seductive

He will stare at again
tomorrow

with religious
longing

NEWNHAM COLLEGE, CAMBRIDGE

(for Inger)

Pensively she sits
by the water lilies
close to where the porter
in a scruffy jacket
stares blankly
at American tourists
who talk about Bufferin
and Madeira.

Brick-red and white-framed
windows –
Sylvia's ghost;
I watch sparrows cavorting
& nymph-like summer students,
barefooted,
walking silently by.

She still contemplates
the beauty of the lily –
the ghost overshadows
forlornly.

GLASGOW

(July 19, 1978)

Woman of Glasgow, your spontaneity
is another fresh wind blowing our way
across this land of heather
highland cows
and massive sheep everywhere.

Rapturous in your greeting –
you extend arms to us along
Sauchiehall Street –
such openness overwhelms.

At the Third Eye Centre
you confide in us about
lover after lover –
remembering one desperately
afraid of the Siamese cat,
then about your cameo role
in *West Side Story* –

Rita Moreno indeed! (Who before
my coming here I'd heard say,
"Me? I could've made it big too,
but I'm Chicano, you see. I'm not
Barbra Streisand, you know.")

In this city there's more than tobacco
and shipping; here's homeliness
and friendliness, laughter
awakening the kindred spirit best.

TWO DANISH WOMEN
(Gairloch, Scotland)

She writes a postcard
her McEwan's Export
almost gone

The other mentions sheep
and more sheep
dotting the landscape
across heather country

Nothing interesting here,
Elizabeth says

Inger bends
her head into a book,
looking down

Atlantic's expanse before us
the glitter of sun
and coruscating waves

At another resort town;
an open snack bar —
the sesame of our evening

Ba-baaing amidst droning cars
            passing by

(July 16, 1978)

SATURDAY NIGHT POEM

It's busy at the club; the men and women
still linger, their insides grown hard
against a thick carapace.

They will remember a time past
with the glass still at their lips,
remembering how they once touched

the stars with crab's pincers, how they opened
doors into the soft ground
and spreadeagled themselves before the waves

whose song was their reason for living.
Becoming one with them for a while,
I hold on to driftwood,

I move according to the moon's neon sign;
I touch the metal sun, dancing
with the beat of lightning,

holding on to you with the urgency
of thunder, as the insects crawl out
of my heart one by one,

and I yearn for the eiderdown
of the sea, warm softnesses
before the night is over.

F. R. SCOTT WALKED IN

I thought he was dead:
he was now like Hamlet's ghost;
a father-figure at eighty,

he nodded, and made a point of law
after the second amendment
at the League of Canadian Poets'
meeting in the City of Saints.

Later he told me he had been
as far as Barbados,
but never Guyana
(let my memory serve me right)

He mentioned Enoch Powell, here
in Canada, and a western politician
wanting to divide this land
like England

I wished I could have read
his palm then –
but I am a quack,
I conceded.

Aloofly,
he understood.

(April 29, 1979)

PARTURITION

Hands born there, feet sticking out
from the greenery
of a chameolonic world;

hurl of feathers
a macaw frenzy
in the midst of more space.

We take turns by the charcoal-
watered creek, we slither and crawl,

we fly again to that blessed country,
yearning for our beginnings.
We splay out our feet –

and the old mother
with hands jutting out, with elbows
bent like the crescent moon,
understands how we feel.

All things meander, bend and turn
all voices are still sharp
before the day dries up
in a rib of sun.

DEATH OF A CONIFEROUS MAN

The tree holds itself rigidly
against the sky;
I walk towards it and slowly
begin the ascent
burrowing into the pith
of wood; I am horizontal now
facing an obscure horizon.
The tree refuses to lean, refuses
to bend: a stalwart tree from beginning
to end, facing ice and cold;
storms too. I burrow further.
I am bird, moving in, touching
more wood, forsaking bark
for the deep, deep inside
where I see nothing else
but absence like a cave.
It's the emblem of what I've
always longed for; I have not
reached the summit – I'm still
inside. Where's the cloud, the sky?
I am horizontal still
as in a death position, and I wait
patiently for the time when I will
release myself –
so help me God, what's this new quest
that I long for, if I continue
to climb higher?

LOOKING FOR GHOSTS

Walking along the Seine, an island in every direction,
suddenly there's rain, and the busy cafés by St. Germain
flaunt those sipping espressos. I ask for 37 *rue de la Bucherie.*
I want to pay homage. You too could be a writer of sorts;
you too could hold the sun under your armpits,
hatching eggs of fire like Guy de Maupassant.

I mumble to the woman walking along with her child;
she replies in Spanish. I curse my lack of French.
Eventually, by Notre Dame Cathedral, I find the bookstore
and enter the wooden building, the clerk telling me
to go meet George, "descendant" of the famous Whitman.
Everywhere in Paris, Americans still abound.

"Yes, you must see him," she insists. "He likes meeting writers."
I walk up the stairs, and patiently wait in the living room.
One blonde youth tells me he's from Alberta, marvels that
I, too, am from Canada. In a corner a woman knits, eyeing me.
I glance around at the titles – all living memorials –
Miller, Hemingway, Anais Nin, Joyce. I suddenly declare
myself a writer. Raised eyebrows all around.

George appears, as if from nowhere, tall, angular,
Lincolnesque, aloof. "All day I've been meeting writers."
He doesn't ask my name, as I wave goodbye.
Downstairs, I jostle anonymous among book-lovers.
A healthy Californian girl saunters in, loudly asks the clerk,
"Do you have a copy of *Les Miserables*?"

(*August 5, 1978*)

SIR JAMES DOUGLAS: FATHER
OF BRITISH COLUMBIA
("What a good a little molasses can do")

1
You were born
where I was born
Demerara's sun in your blood,
Guiana's rain on your skin.
You came from creole stock
taking a native wife
who hardly shadowed
your British pride
with the *dougla* taint.

You're part of my heritage too
despite colonialism
and bending to the rule
for a while.

2
Fever on the Fraser river now:
Victoria's ribbed veins
pulsating with gold-lust.

Settle dispute after dispute
with the Haidas;
sweet smell of molasses
in their veins,
rum dizzying
their minds
while each jewel
formed the dung-
heap of another
claim.

They come from
everywhere now.
Ah, keep the Americans
out, let the rabble
stay far and wide
(de Cosmos, loudest of all).

3
El Dorado of a different kind now.
Note the natives coming
out of their dark days
after the era
of the Hudson Bay Co.
and colonial administration

and I remember pouring
sugar in my tea
in St. Mungo's city
where you were educated,
thinking if you were
more Scottish
I'd be less of the tropics.

from

HEART'S FRAME (1979)

AFTER TODAY,

how else can I offer you praises
in the sun? The fish without scales,
palpitating breath, the spiracles
of health & a chlorophyll beginning
make me less inclined to extol you
before you endanger the species.

I grow up, I watch the rain coming down
with thundering beasts that crowd
the fields: horses on squelchy ground,
cattle in wild commotion – their eyes
more than lightning – sheep bleating
a selfish music.

On this chaste ground they run around
with inflated lungs, they stretch bladder
and pig skin, they drop hair like petals on grass.

We endure the heat, touching on soft ground
where rivulets begin to seep; we long
for more space
                as I sit down to write this,
offering praises on pelt – the words
etched on fat stretched out
against the rim of the sun.

RAMPARTS

In a pretext of sky
he looked at the moon for signs
and arabesques

seeing instead landscape patterning
itself after the clouds
hoping then for sun
in the frenzy of his eyes.

On firm ground roots shoot out
meeting at the zenith of bark
and skin

teeth rocked hard
moon's softness became the respite
that he longed for

the sea took on the fury
with silt and loam
the barricades opened
one long night.

ANYTHING CAN HAPPEN

in a dream:
dreaming about monkeys
that stand and stare,
you wonder what forest
they come from.

Not the same tropical
hinterland
where monkeys litter,
and suddenly there are scores
staring at you.

Feed them bananas;
watch them take on
the shape of the holy
man of Indian lore,
reminding us of evolution's
mystery: how man from
worms can fly
and leap; but all this
may be in a dream.

Besides, dreams can turn
monkeys into snarling
jaguars battling for flesh,
and you wake up expecting
carnivores' spattered blood
all over your bed.

WAKING UP

Waking up early
this morning
hearing now
pigeons badgering
in the eaves
like fidgety
old women
punctual as
alarm clocks
reminds me
of a grandmother
arthritic
and insomniac

A LEGEND

There's a man who knows the seasons
at his finger tips
who holds the sky at a tilt

who watches the rain tumble
with one word land fallows
whole fields blossom

he offers the hearts of fishes
to salvage love
he stares with an ancient glare

his tongue whipping fire
he sits back acknowledging
all things, this godhead man

he's in the bone marrow
beating in the blood
he's enshrined in us all

VACATION
for Len

A prawn memory
by the seined sea

water rising
we furl along

roll with the waves
our clothes on

trade winds lashing
shrimp our eyes

skin crab
we are one

with the sea
breathing salt

our tongues raging
scales of love

SOLID LIGHT

for Arnold Itwaru

The night opens its pages
to us and we are the sun again;
we fan the flames from the recesses
where the waves once highlighted
the drama of our lives

We begin this correspondence
of souls
we rock hard
opening ourselves to wounds –
only dreaming salves us

and each day the fire rises higher
pulses beat with frenzy
restlessly we wait for the words
to come again –

all openings into the solid light.

SHOWPIECE

In the Leicester newspaper
a handsome Indian youth
from South Africa attending
the city's polytechnic
smiles happily
being married now
to the city's Justice
of the Peace's daughter.

Her strong face sculpted in this photograph —
she's determined to have her man —
her father no doubt imagining
a black ram (or brown) tupping
his white ewe, the making
of the beast with two backs.

Oh, the races must mix,
the father sighs.
On the stage will be a hybrid breed —
while he sleeps
a soliloquy in the night's
heavy breathing.

ONE NIGHT STAND

I remind her of the youth in Paris, she says.
I have the same mouth, teeth, and eyes.
I recall the places in her heart; I evoke
feelings like the impassioned rage
she understands. I hold on to her while
the music continues all around,
the others making much ado about much.
She continues to talk after the first kiss –
of a father who walks around in the nude,
a girlie magazine in his hands – they don't mind,
they're used to it, it's always been like that;
of a sister barely sixteen hooked on dope;
a brother, half-hearted homosexual –
all in vain.

Next morning she leaves,
and I'm still wondering
if it's the same girl.

You were pebble and stone,
granite your teeth,
face stalagmite, eyebrows solid
below a ridged forehead,
a stone tablet
in my heart to remember by.

FAREWELL

putting it mildly
when blue sky
is ceiling
and dreaming
in the air without
the usual turbulence
we part, whispering
and imitating acts
saying goodbye
over and over again
like cloudscape
like the hazy
horizon gone astray
from the vantage point
of high altitude
with the heart like
a pressurized cabin
feeling and yet not
feeling the ways
of parting

TAKING A DIVE

There are some things
you always do carefully:
like look among the green
opaque vegetation
like an island –
alligator flowers
unleashing blades
in the virulent sun.

Note the steady glare
from eyes ubiquitous
in daylight,
like embers
during the night,
then wait for
the wild commotion,
the nightmare splashing
of a board-stiff tail.

Remember the ritual fire,
how a reptile
curled like black-sage
leaf on the brick-red
road of a long-gone past.

Clothes peeled off,
softwater, creekwater,
here I come.

INTERSTICES

Seeing through
the interstices
of your thin skin

on mudbank
quivering fish
as big as hands

reflecting
moonlight on water
glaring suddenly

before the eyes
shimmering wet scales
like quicksilver

breathing –
healthily alive

VAMPIRE

In my mother's life
there's a vampire
overtaking us all.

She appears
in the kitchen
early one morning

pulling up her skirt
exposing a fine-grained thigh
showing us purple marks

where the mouth sucked.
I keep looking out
for lurid tongues,

I note grimaces
on everyone's faces,
I talk in my sleep

expecting a vampire's reprieve.
Then with crusted chalk
mother marks

a sign of the cross
daring a vampire
to enter her life again.

Her thigh is safe
for a while
under a pleated skirt.

CROSSING

I say this now
it's like a show
outside memory

you wish to return
forgetful
of the waking up

eyes shunting
the living reality
faces turned away

we will survive
the crossing
it holds no barriers

still it comes
before us
like a mirage

we understand
the contempt
in our lives

we will go back
once in a while
opening our hearts

not to perfect
hate – only
conquering selves

is all I ask now

JUMPING OVER THE MOON

Not any cow can do it.
A farmer's cow does not
have wings; only a specially
winged cow can take off
from the ground, bound through
space like a spaceship
jumping over the moon
(landing on the udder side)

A pneumatic cow
you might say
ballooning its way
through the air

We stare with children's eyes
gullible from the day
we were born,
hoping to see a real cow
coming down,
to watch a real tail
whisking
in the air;
to hear a real moo-cow
mooing from above;
only gravity keeps
pulling it back
to earth

Suddenly we realize
it's merely
a copulating cow,
a farting cow,
a shadow moon
reflected on water,

how Cutteridge
can make some butcher's
cow suddenly jump
over the moon.

from

ELEPHANTS MAKE GOOD STEPLADDERS (1982)

RHAPSODIES

An uncle tries his best
to break out in madness
An aunt reshapes her life
with three children and more

A mother carries in her womb
her thwarted desire
she stitches portions of her skin
with each new child being born

I am somewhere in the loud notes
throbbing in the old brain
I haunt the folds of night
insisting that all is well

I collect discarded bones
to stop the gaps of my nightmare
I bang on the empty drums
                         alone

MAHOUT

Tramping through
the thicknesses
I am the mahout
of my dreams

I welcome elephants
like Newlove's insects
crawling up his legs

I scratch a nose
looking around
overshadowed by
something else

I tramp along
into a bog next
elephant with me
still

and bending down
I react to this
Wild Kingdom
in my life

I make amends with
heavy breathing
being one
of the blind

LOOKING FOR TIGERS

I don't do it often but
I'm somewhere in the garden
where it is not all green

as in your regular orchard
I am reminded of a father's jaunts
in the tropical wilderness

I imagine him digging
holes in the ground
to trap tigers

but tigers are elusive
as in dreams
each night

I see another
I hear a snort
a grunt next

Father comes home
looking weary,
dismayed

a bull bellows distantly
in the folds
of a nightmare

I am the striped pelt
I fall into a trap
of my own making

but I am soon up again
like the river's swell
along the coast

spreading out among the green
I continue to devour
my own flesh

I talk to myself in grunts
I sleep fitfully
in the morning I realize

my father is gone once more
as in a childhood
hide-and-seek game

ELEPHANTS MAKE GOOD STEPLADDERS

It isn't the same growing up
on a different side of the tropics –

after all they're worlds apart,
even though I've been accustomed to hearing

about India's tigers –
not elephants.

How I wished for more than youthful
visits to circuses in a colonial town,

to hear a real elephant's grunt,
to watch its trunk come alive,

to climb with stepladder-ease
as if I'm in the heart of the jungle –

this more than TV Wonderland or Disneyworld.
The trunk lifts up, lowers;

water pours out as if from the clouds.
With Shakuntala innocence

I experience the thrill of monsoon magic;
hands folded, I contemplate the subcontinent's

pastime flood; bending forward,
water at my knees,

I meet the elephant
eye to eye.

ACROBAT

Jumping over the moon
from an elephant's back
does not make for good art

but imagining alligators
at your feet –
twisting and grunting

can cause you to straddle
sideways
while the hide heats up;

and as your body splays out
against a boa-constrictor's trunk
you try to grapple at a ribbon

dangling from the moon;
next you laugh,
believing you are

a pneumatic balloon
hovering above a safari,
trundling along

with bwana shouts;
so you sit rajah plump
and write poems

that stem from the heart

WEAVING FABLES

I.

I am Mowgli, Kipling's
native boy,
the howl of centuries
yet to come.

I am the Bengal tiger, too,
eyes emblazoning
with the outlines
of your face –
solid light in the cave.

Etchings of memory,
body's heat;
the cotton sea heaves
far from Bombay.

II.

On squelchy ground
the monsoon rain
slaps hard, as the cattle
keep winding home,
dogs ululating
as a baboon
loudly coughs.

From a spotted window
I persist,
looking for a change of pace –
being near the Arabian
Sea once again.

III.

Astride a dolphin, I am
my own muse,
contemplating a humpbacked whale,
images carrying me further
in time:

the Middle Passage
as I taste sugar,
my molasses tongue
being all
with the shangrila
of a new sun;

a plantation life,
living in the hovel
I conspire with –
all in a country's
despair.

Crows keep flying low,
circling a tenement
far from Calcutta.
The lotus-eater's dream
is a salve
as I sit close to you

etching vermilion rays,
ringing out a sun's revolution,
my kama sutra body
being all I am left with

as I reach out for a tourist
romance –
palm trees yet swaying,

while I swallow rum and press
my ears to the ground,
genuflecting,
my bones walking out,
with blood gushing –
seeds ready to germinate
a new orchard.

FOR THE SUN-MAN

In the Sun-Man's silence
I walk along,
I am myself jambu
and other exotic fruits

though I do not
pluck parables
from the Buddha's
core

or wonder at ploughing
through the snow
with Hannibal's
beasts.

Ah, being too much
of the west,
the metaphors have dried
like rind

New ones have to be created
while I continue
to cherish
the sun from afar,

thinking
of rainforests
from time to time
in the poem's

winter.

DESIRE

In this imaginary
dream, I itch
with frenzy.
I fight off the fur
scattered on the ground
like roses –
black, black

A mouth puckers;
I am the longing
of the inside, groping
in the dark

With canine frenzy
I mutter a song,
then bark at the gate
with Scylla and Charybdis,
echoing myself hollow

And in the lost time
of paws outstretched
bones broken, breaking
at the sternum

I enter the kennel
of my own making
while morning appears
with scratch marks
on scattered grass

HOW TO SAVE A LIFE

This is the night
when the lungs are intact,
the heart no longer
in frenzy. Bones do not
walk out by themselves.

Together we meander
along the corridor of the skin,
make designs all across
the body.

I offer you solace
with words carved, entrails
coiled in. You give me a tame
life in exchange.

I listen at the navel
for the beasts that still rage,
that keep knocking
against flesh.

LASTING

I am the rat's tail
monster in my own head
mirroring the past

I continue to imagine
doors locked
bodies pressed
against each other

I walk around
with furry feet
grounding myself
in grass

Music of the scampering
night, things moving
swiftly

I hurl around
with top speed
one picture less
of myself

memory of fur
and brownness
I consider the rhythm
of a brown heart,
brown body –

life's lasting
memory

AFTER PABLO NERUDA

"Peasants and fishermen, miners and smugglers,
remained true to their own rough life, to
continuous death and the everlasting resurrection
of their duties, their defeats."
Memoirs

To be a hero
in undiscovered
      territories
is to be obscure:
      these territories
and their songs
      are lit only
by the most
      anonymous
          blood
      and by the flowers
      whose name
nobody
      knows

MARTINS
(for Tom)

Observe a man's delight
in birds —
purple martins in his backyard.
He counts them, notes
their readiness
for flight.

With wingspan, the males
go off first
the females a little later
leaving forty-one baby martins
behind
learning how to fly

dipping over his swimming pool
going over Boo-Boo's head —
ah, the cat's tied
& pulling at his chain
all ruffled

I wonder about bird's delight
as they meander
in their low clumsy flight
until that time when they too
are ready to take off
as if by some weird fate
or instinct

they must leave the north
and head for
South America
to survive the winter's
onslaught.

KEEPING IN TOUCH

I have acquired
two hearts
a dozen lungs
I swallow rocks
and whole trees
from time to time

My teeth jut out stiffly
words are pellets
I play a game accordingly

I press fingers
against my eyes
blotting out the sun
I am in a frenzy
more than once

I take everyone
by surprise
I walk from morning
to night, a mask on,
keeping always
to myself

I, ARCHIPELAGO

I.

I renew old acquaintances
I talk about the past
politicians wrangling
& the gift of rhetoric

The hot sun scorches
all this happening
in one life time –

same old song, quoting
Caesar, and the lust for power.

II.

The islands are small,
yet the violence
the shouts of murder

I look around,
uncomfortable; human nature,
you say, grimacing.

We sip rum, talk about
Jamaica's mannish water;
then laughter.

Looking back from distance
how the world in us
fulfils itself less

III.

I write poetry once again
and dwell on disaster,
the deathbed rocking me

like a bomb blast
while roses grow further
metaphors in my head.

from

ISLANDS LOVELIER THAN A VISION (1986)

LEGENDS

I.

I begin my book of legends
to be other than I am.
I walk across the high bridge,
barefooted in the blistering sun.
I swelter, seeking shelter
from overhanging trees.

Dismay follows with a young
bull bellowing; my father's lasso
converges. He looks back
as I imagine an outside life –
fishing in Ontario, skiing down
Vancouver mountains –
from glossy magazines.

I am still on the winding path
looking for retreat once in a while.
I continue to be livid
I take further note of the sun.

II.

Later in Canada, amidst deciduous
trees, I test myself: I am in a
muskeg, hounded by blackflies
and mosquitoes. I plant tree after tree.
I brace against the cold in northern
Ontario – freezing one more time.

III.

In Kingston I am a founding father
living up to treaties; I bolster
with the old fort: I nurture defence
with brittle skin and flesh;
I grimace as guns keep
firing in my head.

IV.

In Ottawa I am Governor General
and Prime Minister, too,
Parliament Hill my domain. I look
around: cannons firing from the past,
relived in my dreams. A burning next.
I continue to listen to entreaties.
War Measures Act. My mind festering
solitudes.

V.

Finally, my mother, to remind me
of myself, sends a postcard from
Tobago – she on her first holiday
after fifty years or more.
I continue to make humming noises
in my sleep

CHANGING

I gather the heat
in all my cells
I forge with every ounce of flesh

I splay out on the ground
scattering organs, blood
everywhere

I gather them up again
for a renewed self
I plaster everything with wax

Suddenly I begin to fly –
I am Icarus
venturing out –

in, then down
as I am still aloft
singing in the tunnels

of my flesh, the corridors
of heart and lungs
in my hollow bones

I moult, bird-like
anew, as never before
heart pulsating –

my future's self
again aloft
in the frenzy of breathing

MY BROTHER IS A HERO

He rummages through the forest
with a passion
he tears whole trees down
with a savagery that is livid in nightmares

He builds chairs, tables, cabinets —
he's galvanized more than zinc
he's the turbulence of tropical sun & rain

he heaves and toils with frenzy
and the forest more than Macbeth's
moves at his command

New things are born from day to day
more trees with arms & legs
he spins the landscape around
he's a maker first of all

with sawdust blood & bones

LENIN PARK, HAVANA
(July 14, 1982)

My camera flashes upon the variegated faces
amidst general activity
of building, establishing.
How eager they are, these hands, bodies –
nine, ten and eleven-year-olds
bustling about without weariness –
only a restrained air of the carnival
of the young
this summer.

I will say *"Hola"*
in bare Spanish,
eager to find out how the socialist man
or woman can transform a state
in command's way. They seem not to mind –
innocence has its own currency as I watch
a young girl driving a tractor,
a boy milling rice; another refining sugar.

Will they ever starve, as they pay tribute
to Jose Marti, Fidel Castro, or whoever else
will lead them?
Or will some stalwart spirit
among them, given to brooding,
high on culture, insist on the right
to be free beyond bread?

Doubtful as I am, I banter, smile;
my camera snaps again, left and right –
black hair bordering beautiful
dark and brown faces – I love you all!
A hybrid breed chockful of Latin air.
Among you, perhaps, are eager dancers,

singers, poets – how elegantly you proclaim
an island in the pulsation of your bodies,
in the greater exaltation of spirit yet to come
far beyond Castro or Marti.

RUM-RUNNING

A Maritimer's new life —
I am at the edge of my seat; water boiling,
mud slaking;

a kiln's turnaround
at the city's end. Fumes rise up
and swirl

across the ocean, Atlantic's swell
and billow. I taste cod
in Jamaica, Barbados, Trinidad
and Demerara — more trade — while in
Newfoundland, later,
I lie drunkenly.

Wind wafting. Whole fields of sugar cane
and beet. Backyard and tenement —
hear the police siren. Now run, man!

An urchin's scampering feet,
shirt tails flying in the wind;
such ragged talk afterwards, scattering
fowls, duck. A goat's lone grunt —

good as a bray. I hold onto a wad of notes
like a tufted beard, dancing my way
to paradise. Half-sotted, I echo disdain
and continue to make believe,

patterning myself whole, dreams coming
alive across an ocean, a ship canting,
land lifting up, the fumes yet in my nostrils,
my body's own heat —
I continue to rise like yeast.

THIS FATHER'S LIFE

This father's life I plunge into
surfacing with the dream of cattle
a hinterland's jaguar-call
a grunt as good as a bray

A coastland voice next
as I am memory of the deciphering madness
I walk around, pulverizing
with distress,

going back with a thousand images,
song of siren, expecting
something new to be born
a calf-head jutting out
a branding three months later

I am the squeal and the running hooves
I am the beast tearing out entrails
from the mouth-shape of a tree
I am the howl against the moon
in a father's sun-absence

where gall and bitter dewdrop
make for memory much too long

THE HUSBAND

After a week
in the town's brothel
he came home
bringing Shamin, the town whore
with him

His fat wife (she was once beautiful
with fair skin)
sat in the kitchen and grumbled
by herself

I, one of the villagers, gossiped
like the rest
while he remained
in the bedroom upstairs
in the house built
on stilts

His wife knew there
was nothing she could do
but wait until his passion
was sated
      with a bottle of rum

She muttered about leaving him
But she never really did –
      "It was bound to happen that way,"
I heard her once say
      to her children

Afterwards he played
      the mandolin beautifully –
his wife laughed
      all by herself.

STILL LIFE

Hear her,
with her lips sealed;
from afar
you could tell she was swinging
a chicken by the neck
with blood squirting from her fingers
like rain

With thunder in her eyes,
she breathed out moonshine
she who could ferret out lightning
by baring her teeth
in the virulent sun

How she laughed –
she was still young then,
full of energy like a young horse.
One afternoon, I remember
she brought home a lover
and wrapped her arms about him
like wet banana leaves

I was under the house
built on stilts, then,
playing Robin Hood & his Merrymen,
amidst tropical sun & rain.
I was also Errol Flynn
making Captain Blood arches
dazzling with a sword
in the guise of skull
& crossbones

DINNER
for Keith Lowe

I.

Responding to your invitation –
the doctor was there – we exchanged
pleasantries, old memories – like being
by a familiar riverside. And the English girl
you talked about – with whom you climbed
Blue Mountain peak – then the hurricane came.
The doctor said he could've done it
with ease, being a Queen's scout, the first
Chinese in the Canadian Armed Forces.

II.

Harvard at eighteen, and what else shaped your life
while I slept in a cardboard-box in grandmother's
cakeshop, with bootleggers all around.
Later, in the American Civil Rights movement
you talked loudest: We're all visible –
your demands, their behest.

III.

Neither of you speak Chinese –
Jamaica's continuing remembrances –
our being here now on Cartier Street in a capital's
downtown winter. We eat salmon and rice;
you, returning to Toronto, then to Jamaica,
again to hear of murder.

I contemplate taking you to a burlesque –
your last night – her navel level with your eyes,
the sheer cornucopia of her thighs
                             in Ottawa.

DROWNING CATS

There is really nothing to it –
it happens in Belfast too, where they
also have their poor;
it's like singing sad songs
with tattered clothes flapping in the wind.

The cats, meowing in the darkness all
night long, awaken a young girl who will
rise early the next morning to prepare food
for her husband to go to the cane-fields;
another kind of whimpering if you like.

The cat's disdain; its eyes widen in the semi-dark,
then emerald and neon; you wait and watch,
fearing the kittens that are soon to be born –
sometimes half a dozen or more. In a year, maybe,
scores will be staring at you in the streets,
as you walk by with fish in hand.

The days go by, the nights whimpering too.
Grandmother would repeat:
"Now there's really nothing to it;
simply put them in a bag and tie the end.
They will not see, they will not remember
how to get back here."

Funnily enough, so often they seem to return,
these same cats, like a haunting, familiar
as old memories.

My girlfriend casually tells me that in Belfast
they also do the same, maybe with a difference;
they tie the bag with a stone
and drown them!

OJIBWAY

Tell me, Larry, who have you conned next,
selling fake Indian artifacts in Toronto?

Another trip back home and still spending
your money on booze in Longlac,

picking a fight with your girlfriend;
she comes after you like a dog.

You make up, fight again;
another long round of booze and depression.

Panhandle for a while; then shoot pool
at Trapper Lake where you are for the season

planting trees; that night beside my bunk
you snored heavily; next morning

you painstakingly made a sandwich,
a dozen slices of bread piled high —

again the artist! The trees by now
have grown tall; the ground still swirls

under your feet; the artifacts will
remain admired, like a dead moose's eyes.

VOZNESENSKY

You, Andrei Voznesensky,
what is Russia all about?
Tell me with fury on your tongue.

Let the Russian words roll out.
Does mysticism
still surround the Russian soul?

You, *tovarish*, tell me why
you're so calm tonight?
Why formalism still means so much to you?

I understand your once
nearly committing suicide,
you, then a dissident.

Now I suppose I forgive your interest
in Margaret Trudeau
being here in Ottawa

(*November 13, 1982*)

DIASPORA

You presume to know
more of the world
than you were prepared for

New York — you transformed
and transforming — breathing
fully, trying to understand
the sum of a life

Making music with your telephone
tongue. Highrises. Cars zooming by.
Night school & getting your B.A.

Standford next. A dream coming true.
You're still a union man
championing workers' rights in the big city

Surprises to follow —
in the familiarity
of memorable colloquialisms

PASSION PLAY

Heart, take me there where I know myself —
take me to the wide rivers once again,
brown the waters, the plying raft,
the shadow of the hand, mighty oars; take me
where I am also the flower bursting out
from a ribbed cage —
the boa-constrictor uncoiling malevolently.

Heart, make me bolder yet, even as I am near hunger,
same as the man who will cry *jump, jump,*
from a high window to find salvation,
the shanty-town deep in his ears.
Help me make a living out of nothing.

Heart, I am the kernel of the coconut-seller's dream.
In this narrow street, in an old colonial town
I offer you a sacrifice: this jelly, precious water,
my blood. I will sate your appetite for a while;
you will not dream of bread any longer
in the darkest night —
all the world's orchards will be ours.

Heart, let me tumble down with rain-clouds,
crossing the river again; looking with rainbowed eyes
I enter a cave here, where I can survive longest,
my spirit whole, body bent, prostrate —
a new beginning. Hear me, oh heart,
help me keep intact the fire in my eyes.

SONATA

I am in the frenzy of another life
I give the village hands and legs

I listen to everyone's surprised
laughter, as I keep talking
in dreams

I fail to understand why I am
like this; I'm held to ransom
once more

eyes and ears next –
no longer mine;
I shout with a loud voice

my heart stops
I turn around and burrow
deeper into myself;

this pact goes on
from day to day
as I continue to live

in bones –
to salvage a life

DUBIOUS FOREIGNER

As there is no doubt
    where I come from

I answer to all the mistrust
    you let out
        onto myself

A dollar-value citizenship card
    bulges out
        against my hide of skin

I repeat history
    to myself
        once in a while —

my feet splayed out
    against a liana sun
        swinging against the horizon

belching out the past
    with Asia & Africa
        in my ears

Next iridescent & emerald
    as the waves
        I acknowledge the pattern

answering to myself
    in Canada
        with crabgrass

on snowy virginal
    ground

ONE MAN'S WAR

Take note: I'm not preternaturally inclined
to believe in the war of human beings;
this is the onslaught, words lashed out at first
as a man vocally extends himself,
prehistoric in stride
and struggling through the dark.

I watch him being wieldy, man with whiskers –
Himmler or Hitler – he breathes hard,
his tongue wagging,
then knotted as in barbed enclosures.
Trapped, death echoes a fulsome rapture–
travesty of an ever-present Belsen or Auschwitz.

He recounts with familiar strides,
kicking our emblems of bones,
his own glamorous ways
dismissing the rest of us. So it appears
to this former soldier, warrior, beckoning all other wars;
his tongue still rolls out thunder.

He prepares himself for the final assault,
throwing his hands above his head, glaring.
He echoes, blasts the rest of us.
He understands the drama of previous wars best.
I aim to outlast him, my quiet's victory
being catharsis from the start.

FAREWELL AGAIN

for Constantine Melakopides

Our blood no longer runs
in the same vein
you hold on to reason
with a passion

I make amends with water falling –
our pith and cambium hearts
no longer relevant. In our
different worlds

you try to decipher
the heiroglyphic concept.
The philosopher's stone
glitters from afar.

We will continue to write letters, brother.
I will again begin
with a farewell song
of praise

All will be well in Canada
until old Athens is ready
to burn her acropolis
because you have stayed
away for so long.

AFTER ROMANCE

for Derek Walcott

Plagued into becoming more of myself,
I travel along this dreamer's path.

Take the world as it is in me;
it is the only real place

as I am unable to conquer more of myself.
This too is epistemology:

the ways of becoming ingrown
like one's toenails

and being reminded of the burnt-brick heap,
the bird alighting,

remnant of a lost paradise.
With a realist's touch, I consider

my father becoming grey,
shaking in his ramshackle bones.

A brother next:
news of an imprisonment.

Another night without sleep:
Oh the ways of keeping vigil,

being the imagination's fugitive!
I scatter grains of rice while insects

scurry across a bed where a nephew
slept the night through.

Now trying to hang the moon from a pillow
with a trade wind's rhythm, I burn

from all sides – feet and brain first.
Making amends, I become the somnambulist,

meandering through the thicknesses,
mythologizing as much as you.

PARTNERSHIP

(or a dream)

I continue to give you arms & legs
Your body holds out against dismemberment
You turn and look at me without a grimace
I offer bandages without so much as an apology

We continue our old game, looking at each other
with myriad eyes from false sockets,
exchanging hearts & lungs.
After a while I put my trophies in a bag
and sling it across my shoulder –

time for the wandering again.
I leave you behind with a look of distress
You follow with a handful of flowers,
your octopus limbs stretching out,
trying to embrace me

And I keep looking back at the sun
shining down upon us; I keep hoping that this
will not last forever. Your tentacled arms
will soon be all around me –

and I begin squirming, disappearing
from life altogether

MAGIC ROBOT

You came into my life
with a shiny newness
answering questions
about the universe

I was only nine
or ten –
but I knew your style
was false

when the arm broke

Then your answers drew blood
I could only be amazed
as the world
was suddenly

without a centre

You spun on glass
like an ineffectual
dancer –
so time went by

marred with upheaval

one-armed
one-armed

WOLFE ISLAND, ONTARIO

You have made a pact
with the lake
as pickerel & pike
come up to round off
your life

For seventy years or more
you breathed
heavily, as the waves
beat against the island

Now the girls attending Queen's
humour you with Maritime jest,
flouncing their shapely
eighteen-year-old bodies
– you continue fishing

They tell you about the boys
in their lives, of riding
around the island
& wishing to take them
by surprise

You smile, ask questions
about the world.
They laugh; you look down
into the lake, seeing all
the knotted things;
rock-bottom for a while,
you imagine a youth –
a life never fully spent

The girls leave now
they enter the ferry,
passing the old fort,
the military college;
you wave steadily,
like an awakened dreamer

When all is gone you empty
your blood & guts into the lake;
the fishes make patterns
all across your life

from

COASTLAND (1989)

ANACONDA'S DOUBT

It turned and made a wave
among bramble and floating twigs;

it heaved with an answer and breathed
heaving against the swirl of the dark;

it did not understand the pinprick
that could make blood ooze, that could

cause dizziness in its head; it remained
coiled and belched fire like a dragon;

it knew its ancestry without knowledge
of Jung – it merely kept its eyes open

and watched other beasts take their turn
to swallow. It heaved for flesh, it snorkled

with an earflap that was missing before.
It moved forward and stretched its body

like tentacles, outdoing an octopus in rage.
It understood the message of viscera –

blood and pulp and algae around its lungs –
it didn't mind; it simply cleared things

out of the way and rested peacefully
in a sluggish mire to grow more cells

that would swallow and absorb; that would
dream how things long past could survive.

ORNITHOLOGY

for Jorge Etcheverry

The hummingbird behind the paleolithic rock;
this eucalyptus dance of paradise.

Loping forward, the hairs on the back of my neck
standing on end – the spirit's flight.

New day, drizzle of rain. In this argument
Huxley can devour you with stopped mouth,

a bishop's bowed head in prayer – all
in the fastness of vines, tangles of undergrowth.

Once more at an angle of flight –
do you wonder at the universe?

Does the sun continue to emblazon
with emerald? Lying quietly, the afternoon

stealing away, the forest all around,
your sex in your hands,

wetness at the corners of the mouth;
a petal wind; logic diffuses the universe.

Clapping my hands, the bird naturally takes to the air!

FOREIGN LEGIONS

This is a surfeit, believe me.
I am circumscribed in the desire to traverse
whole landmarks, this rage in me
as I am scuttled or going beyond.
Now cockeyed because of hibiscus or bougainvillea,
I contain myself with a tropical burning.
This too is belief; the spirit harks at luminosity,
the sun itself leaping forward in the constancy
of rain, the slush of fewer days around,
the weather falsifying grass,
the squelch critical as syllogism.

Thrilled by the furore of other days,
other longings, a strange madness takes over.
The sun in a myriad of rivers in the late afternoon –
how splendid the lakes, alluvium of a special kind!

I gather all the selves mirrored in the display
of leaves, and one moment is more fragmentary
than all the others, as water again scuttles,
displaying ripples like oblivion.

Now I hold on to a stopped mouth, ear;
I am vanquished for a while as I sit down
at the edge of the forest and talk in tongues
of silence, mirroring other longings.
Take me, I say, to the butterfly's wings,
the world itself welcoming me as I am
the imagination's leap and spirited blood.

Disaster comes soon after, and I am stuck
in one place; I am hailed from afar, standing tall,
both feet splayed out, Moongazer,
whirling with shadows, without anxiety.

Let the dreams take over, let the tides
vanquish all others while I wait
for the rebirth far ahead –
the moment's mammoth start.

MY COUNTRY, NORTH AMERICA, AND THE WORLD

With a dune of sugar the imagination
licks itself; the heart beats faster;
the Middle Passage's below deck.

With Raleigh at the Orinoco, take me as I come,
indentured or indigenous.
Whose world?

Again crossings: the new rises up;
I am a Parliamentary breed, lurching forward
with Canning, Buxton, Wilberforce –

the dark's passing passion.
Now the Great White North, striving
for the albino state, I will soon be perfect

without piquancy. What's ahead of us?
It is you I fear most, you who I
think of constantly,

falling prey to deeper sins, far beyond
the commandments. Blindfolded,
covered with blood.

Let me walk a straight path,
let me come to you with only
a sharp tongue.

Let me reach those limits where
I will protest only with the cry
of peace,
                              finally.

INTERLUDES

(for Craig Tapping)

The woman in the library, in her twenties,
reads zealously, searching with her eyes
the bones of the page, blood of gremlin her nose,

longing for tidbits of where she comes,
from what Maritime place. Here now in this Haida
country, the sea lingers in her blue-and-white collar.

Newfoundland or Nova Scotia, what does it matter?
A time of rum-running. Meanwhile, I imagine
cricket galore, reading the CLR James' column

in the London *Times,* scoring divisions and subdivisions,
boundaries in my mind, entertaining Catholic whites –
DeVenterul, De Gannes, De la Bastide.

I make further strokes as I watch middle-class browns
and blacks, those running faster down the pitch;
a mighty spring next, throwing the ball like the tide.

Such a time when local players or even a woman
in the nineteenth century could organize a tour of England,
or Canada. Yes, take some Blacks who could bowl faster!

Woman, your friendly looks, eyes, invite me to indulge
this pastime of reading, in this rage
of runs and homesickness.

ROCK HARBOUR

for Sylvia Plath

I.

A dead-end corner,
cul-de-sac;
two jugs of milk
for the children please.

A cold winter morning;
upstairs the old man
is knocked out by the fumes.

The Australian girl hammers
at the door, eager
to enter the death-womb.

I will face up to the demon
bearing witness to the endgame,
pouring milk down the drain.

II.

The winter tree stands sentinel
in the graveyard, shadowing
the man who walked along Rock Harbour.
Such a dark vampire sucking the blood
dry, licking the marrow clean.

You cross the water of death,
listening to the sirens, pale
sisters of stone. They pull you down,
down into the underworld
O Persephone!

III.

The little god is a horse
bolting across the blue,
you foam to wheat in a glitter
of seas, rising up suddenly
to your wildest glory,
fumigating first with the Jews
at Auschwitz and Belsen in the chambers
of death; Mother Earth's singed pubic hairs;
a bowdlerised Lazarus without balls.

Thank God for large mercies –
a cornucopia of turkey neck and gizzard
anatomised in a laboratory
where babies flounder in vinegar.

IV.

I will resurrect with you after
the feet-washing and anointing
are over. Gather azaleas from the dim
cemetery and watch you blink
at thalidomide babies bobbing
in the green sea of memory.

AS AN IMMIGRANT,

I have made out of Canada
bones, sawdust, fire engines,

fuel, the ground reshaped into tunnels,
as I am here with a vengeance.

This too is flesh, making arrangements
as I dramatize with the spirit, my way,

watching railway tracks, sleepers
in my midst, chug-chugging along.

How steel leaps I will never know.
I am at the edge of mighty lake

Superior, bound by water, trees,
sand, other lakes, the ground swirling.

Let the beaver bring me closer
as I quarry silence and talk

in riddles that the maple leaf
itself will finally understand.

TRAVELLING

Looking back from afar, in this appearance
of hippie culture, the Canadian National Railway

uprooting sleepers and chug-chugging along;
time's drone in Nanabijou's city;

the Sleeping Giant resting hands on a boulder,
heavy as Mount McKay.

I chase after the wind in Nipigon;
an Ojibway boy's bird mightily slaps

the rock, wings beating in my own heart –
this frenzy alive with the train's speed.

Time to outlast, Rip van Winkle now,
I look back into the western sky,

telling the mightiest of lakes to echo
more of the wind. I walk a straight path,

my patched jeans flapping
against an ankled summer.

APPRAISAL

Conjuring up romance with hopes and fears –
mannerisms we call advocacy or racial assertiveness –

the ethnics taking over – we cry out vengeance,
marvelling at the roots of trees,

the workers constantly hacking off the limbs of elm.
Along Sussex Drive the noise of the waterfall is all.

Boundaries, oceans, a mighty river's swell;
whitefly foaming; your black hair hanging down,

legs wide open and welcoming love:
this rendezvous with the ethnics, their potency

and other desires like unaccustomed rain –
eager as I am to populate a country –

colour is still all. Try thwarting a rainbow
at odd hours, this melting pot or mosaic,

Mackenzie King still our guide, and trembling
at the hands of fascists, the gates of Parliament

opening. Gunpowder too has its limits. I say
walk along Rideau and Bank Streets

or watch the natives pointing to the bear
in the sky or telling false tales to the spruce

and jackpine close to Sioux Lookout and Longlac,
reforesting a country after a fire,

partridges hopping in the wooded dark!

STREETS

These too are streets, journeys, places that I
hide in, that I shout out with a loud voice.

I say, *Do you understand that memory cannot disappear?*
Give me the maple leaf and I will show you the veins,
as I cry out emblems from far-off places.

Can you swim undersea? Can you tell one planet
from the other? Same voyages – I am
Irish too, thrashing in a potato famine.

In my many voices I keep coming to you,
at the edge once more as I shout out the land.
Do not leave me empty; the streets are still bare.
I crouch and bend, I carry imprints   my name   my name.

God, this is all I ask! When the land
says it is temperate,
I am eager for it to be otherwise.
I say marvellous things, asking that
together we haul stones, boulders; we will build
across the terrain in British Columbia
Quebec   Ontario   the Prairies   Newfoundland.

Districts of the North, I come to you,
I love you all the best.
I love you   you.

SEAFARER

I am a crouching, low, misshapen,
born-under, sheep-belly creature
wishing to take you by surprise.

I have wandered in more
than a cave, mingling
with dank clay, dried grass,

more smell of sheep
as I am part wool
evading your Cyclopean eye.

I look for open space
with memory of oceans,
whirlpools,

my head spinning –
bracing against the pelt
once more,

bolts of lightning
locked in my forehead,
as I wish you

to see me through
as I am still being
hurled, moving about

Ulyssean. I splay out
breathing in fully
at the entrance

ba-baaing, my jutting out
ear's accompaniment,
the horizon's Athena

afar

FOR COLUMBUS

I.

When grapes are her breasts
and apples her skin, I am at home.
I long for Italian brothers, Greek sisters,
an African father
        an Indian mother.

I long with the same longing
as the clouds coming down, the sky
about to tilt over
like a ship in a hefty sea.

I long too for a French aunt
who will elegantly raise her a handkerchief
in the wind, signalling an archipelago
as I cry out, "Islands, islands!"

II.

Now it is you who I remember,
your neck bruised, the shadow
of an axe coming down
in the Tower.

You too, Cortez, as Montezuma burns
inside, his cry resounding in the night;
you with your Quetzalcoatl face,
a helmet still glinting.

        Pizarro next,
as I watch the Incas in silver mines
living out a life, buried in sand, their heads
above the ground while the ocean once more
threatens disaster.

III

With a Crusoe mask, I listen in the distance;
our Friday commands,
the Spanish Empire sinking in the background.
This treasure is all I am left with,
Bible in hand, the sun whipping by,
a lopsided moon sinking lower
        into the bottomless sea.

As I try to jump over it, my *paradiso,*
El Dorado, the heathen sky
falls prostrate
        at my feet.

from

STONING THE WIND (1994)

PRETENCES

These are my
contributions;
it is a form
of magic

I begin with
an exchange
of the body
combining

with the elements:
earth first
water next.
I take fire

from your hands
you pretend
to shake out
air from your elbows

All is well
with the world
as we conjure up
spirits with ease

The alchemist in us
makes a declaration
of independence
as we are free

DESIRES

I.

I have desired other things: paradigms,
complexes. I have talked my way through
spheres, stars, whole clusters of leaves
on a sidewalk of overwhelming elm.
I pride myself upon hearing voices of birds,
convinced that they dart, come after me;
it is the hypotenuse, the angle of a matrix.
I recover and cling, or scuttle in water
here by Lake Mississippi, watching bass
in throes of death; and the hockey-player boys
are good at it really; they boast to their parents
as the boat comes in full throttle –
all 60HP of it!

More desires, like plain talk, like eating corn
bought off a huckster along the Carleton Place
roadway, and barbecued chicken this August,
my chipped tooth still benign; and Cassidy,
the only girl in the family – the only one who plays
hockey on the boys' team – smiles and shows off her
trophies. She wears pink, her hair long; her mother,
with suppressed glee, says none of the boys
bodychecks her. Paedophile! Stratagems carrying
a huge smile like fishbone,
my being conversant with stars; ripples
in water; memory refurbished.
Bill, the former NHL player, is now telling us
about the Carleton University students at the cottage
who run around naked all summer. It's a sight
to behold. Cassie grimaces.

II.

Myrna talks about the children once more:
how it will all pay off one day – having all
winter to drive the boys twice a week to Ottawa
and back – and how proud the children really are
since they make it a point to tell the others
that their father was once in the NHL –
hockey being all.

       And Bill, remembering that while
in the NHL he had an apartment all to himself
in New York, though he played for the Leafs,
but his knee was smashed after being bodychecked
heavily – and now the desire is gone.
That was how it was though, he says to his own
father, a United Church Minister, small-framed,
amiable, who suddenly swings with a golf club.
It's all nerve-wracking, Bill adds; but now he's
devoted to his auto sales outlet, and an inventory
turnover is all that preoccupies him these
days – to his death, Myrna quickly says.

III.

The children, craving for sun, laugh as I am
still meshing with stars, planets, the speedboat's
throb in full throttle, a dive when all other
solutions fail. Complexes take over, like salt
in water – and the nude ones at the cottage,
so ample in the delectable air. Skating down the
sideboards, the puck slaps hard against a girl's
face, but Cassie, only seven years old, defends;
while Myrna, thirty-five, cheers on from the sides,
as the others wonder at the power of birds rising

155

to scatter the ground like atoms.
Other desires make me jolt with a knee pain,
and like Bill, I say it's the worst one can
encounter, one's body stretching to a snapped
spinal cord.

Fish in water, or flowers by the roadside,
convulse or congeal: laughter still being all,
barbecuing this summer with people I never knew before,
whose lives suddenly become mine, etched,
imprinted like children's feet,
charcoal residues in my heart.

WIDOW

You will live up
to an agreement
to go out and walk
in the woods
around Kingston

Among widows
all is not well –
thigh-beats
and heart flaps
at night.
Now is the time
once again, sister,
for tramping through
vines & evergreens

Or do you still remember
a marriage of sorts –
regret or sorrow
all elusive as dreams?

Everything is changing.
You will continue
to make garlands
of all other people's lives
but your own

So, drink apple
and cider juice
on a farm;
walk home, and leave
the musk of someone
else's past
far behind

NOTHING LIGHTS UP

for Joy Kogawa

Under the oak tree
    they sit
old as they are
    hardly speaking.

Only gestures
    in the consummation
of these final
    years.

    Love. The wind.
Sun and rain. A fly squats
    nearby.
Takes off again.

Their eyes unravel
    secrets
of an oriental path.
    Lips pucker,
slightly.

    Smoke swirls
in the leap
    of understanding –
this marriage
    lasting fifty years
or more.

In silence
    they mesh
the voices
    of their skin.

BY LAKE MINNEWANKA
(Banff National Park)

I.

We're feeding mountain sheep
or goats — what does it matter?
We're asking them to be good citizens,
or simply to be at their best, while
Rolf, camera in hand, zooms in,
quickly saying, "Get the horny one"
with aldermanic zest; he's priest-like,
lips throbbing over the aesthetic
quest upon this natural scene
here in highland Alberta, Lake Placid
mirroring a semblance of lust or
lofty pleasure.

Diane and I are still feeding the sheep
chocolates. "Sure thing, get the horny one,"
Rolf says. "Feed them nuts as well."
From inside the car, images distort
Calgary's distant yet concrete spread.

II.

The sheep take off after a while,
and politicians like truants
hurl themselves into the nearby brush
to start hiking, leaving me to mull
upon the lake's crest, while other
visitors come by from time to time.
I am now the silent hunter, a grove
all around: jackpine with hooves suggesting
imminence of danger far away from Ottawa.

A dog appears, taking after the sheep –
a dozen of them at once – and the Native
coming out of his camper, his girlfriend close by,
laughs with distorted pleasure as the dog
snarls – such ferocity in hot weather.
The sheep plunge deeper into danger.
It's what's left now, the vehement strides
with blood flowing, wool and flesh scraped
from bone, all the horny ones really, desire
still making us survive in the wilderness
where "nature red in tooth and claw" assures
of yet another life, if bye-laws or fiercer love
by politicians, hardbooted and crushing leaves,
will less dramatically allow.

MAD WOMAN OF HARVARD

As if flies are after her,
she flits incessantly
with a thin-leafed book,
this woman, grey-haired,
a long brown coat draping

her frail body. She walks
swiftly to another tree,
swats, then struts off again,
waging her wars; she turns,
looking around,

seeing me, she with fierce eyes,
my spirit oddly in tune with hers.
A couple close by also look at her,
amused at her cryptic smiles, Eumenides
dogging her path. The mind's weakness,

I say, my own, with this longing for knowledge.
She cries out deep inside at the dim sun's
rays. "You there, it's no good watching
other people – you in the dark glasses!"
A scholar's grimace, all on green grass

splayed out as I am, alert
to other traumas, other worlds, as
she keeps marching up and down,
all words waywardly expressed, if you must
know, or keep thinking about, always.

(*Harvard University Campus, August 1986*)

TAKE ME OVER

Take me over, draw me in;
  make me a slave to paper and ink.
Believe in me as in the days past,
  this clock's hour; oh, the ways
of conjuring up the rainbow
  at the river's bend.

Laughter with paper rolling,
a tongue hanging out. Wind ruffles
  the palm of my hand, your voice on the phone –
  the lone caller stalking the night,
as we share secrets from a common source.

  This midnight of more meetings,
or an arrangement really with laughter –
  in Ottawa where I have come
to live out life, bit by bit,
  watching the clock strike the hour
with a temper of its own as I get ready
  to berate all others, my mouth
sucking in air, my last gasp
  at the edge of the sea –
    where else?

The desk talks back to me, the paper folded,
  the typewriter humming;
alphabets crushing against one another –
  other tales too far away,
like quaint voices,
  quainter yet as I recall all other hates,
or distant fervent loves.

MOON'S PIETY

The moon objects to her assaults
during the day, keeping track
of her fingers, hair, eyes.
She's bone-thin this summer;
her blood does a false run-around.
Her heart withers from outside.
The moon begins a recovery course,
assembling all the bones together;
they nurture the stars with a piety,
discussing a strategy for action.
They walk about in the open fields,

tracing the steps of other women
who come out with a chorus, who
exchange flowers and tell stories
of the active life. The night
appears before them with a fanfare;

all is well in the world;
the stars take over without so much
as an apology. She sits down and begins
her attack upon life, the ground
swirling under her feet.

And the moon sits back aloofly,
witnessing all this from her balcony
of clouds, doing her rounds with
a beating heart, wishing for her
a life without frenzy or regret.

THE REVEREND LUKER

Dobson's "Cynara" in your veins – no other;
you pull with a saw, hammering a further cathedral
in our midst, a colonial town's foundry.

Watching you steadfastly with a romanticism
all my own as you establish murder once more
with a practised voice, Beckett's BBC elocution

or tape-recorder's hum, close to the pulpit;
the commands you gave, inspiring us with words
of praise, or pushing us to the limit at the Teachers'

College with Shakespeare and other stalwarts
amidst frogs croaking, crickets cheeping
in ghostly New Amsterdam – an alligator's cough

coming from the darkwatered Canje creek,
the wider Berbice not far away, winding
in the night's stygian blackness. In quest

or disbelief with other shapes and shadows –
Mittelholzer too hailing us from afar –
sawdust in your eyes, the hammer at your sleeves,

you stirred us with the anthem you created,
"Green Land..." and forged ties with England –
more than Raleigh ever could.

GRANDMA'S GRAMMAR

I.

It is a quick message with words, emblems,
this tropical beginning or plantation frenzy

eclipsed now as I talk to you, or listen,
mouth puckering – swear words really;

rage in the heat with the nerves gone
haywire; the mouth's further twist or tongue's

quest, lips throbbing in the potpourri of memory.
Other ruins: an old fort, Kyk-over-al, indenture,

Demerara or Orinoco: further rivers in me,
the words cracked like clay, alluvium and topsoil.

II.

The wedge of language, the lexicon rephrased,
or sheer hourglass rhythms

beating a leaden tongue. A barbed
presence is all as I mutter on because

of a subcontinent's clutter or lore. An elephant
somewhere next; then a Bengal tiger.

Heaving with false breath, mind's metamorphosis,
we decorate words with more acts in the sun,

the verbs' wood and pith, the nouns' renowned logic
now part of heritage, or mere figures of speech in Canada.

III.

Grandma sneers in the quiet, having never really left,
never known other islands, archipelagoes, never seen

peninsulas like a mirage when this same language suddenly
seals her lips, her tongue still stretching like barbed wire,

or twisting a refrain with the selfsame Irish, Scottish,
Welsh – cockney inhabiting her breath – despite Hindi...

Other emblems I continue to live with
in the tundra at this time of the year – perennials.

I watch distantly with eyes fixed on the past, the present
browbeating us because of what I long to hear – and will not.

THE DRIFT
for Rea

Here's a death,
a brother's
body poison

reaching out,
the heart
in flight.

Viscera's
changeover –
after cremation

& scattering
the ash
in Canje's waters.

Memory hurts
after a while,
living out

a lost life –
killing the blood
of time.

MARABUNTA

It will sting you and make you never want to fall asleep;
your eyelids will swell quickly
in the sun, the red blaze, the pain

coming after you; it will chase you for miles
as you run faster, in the hollows, wanting to go underground
in some cave, maybe,

or meandering through brush, grass, vines,
escaping it as it comes again after you,
attacking with fury;

and you dared to disturb its nest
under the tarpaulin of black sage leaves,
hibiscus, zinnia, in the sun's unrelenting eye.

The wasp hasn't given up yet, it will attack
one more time. You wait and see, watching
from gables, roof top, mango and coconut tree.

It will seek you out, zooming in, clinging to your hair;
it will seek revenge, make merry with the pain
in your face, forehead, eyelids again,

your head dizzy with the tremors
of blood vessels broken,
bulbous eyes looking back at you

– our own Eumenides!

THE BIG APPLE

I have decided to be cheerful;
on Fifth Avenue, I lost
twenty dollars in a card game.

I, who felt I was smart,
fell into such a trap,
mesmerized by the sleight of hand.

Now, back at my own game,
responding to words only,
I wait here by the New York City Library,

thinking how best to pursue my craft,
mulling over passers-by,
the old man chasing after a youth –

"Stop him!" he cries.
A few feet away, a woman
reads Marquez; asks her boyfriend

if he knew him
and what solitude conveys
to the rest of us. I consider

metaphor like distance –
the forest floor of a city
swirling in the summer's heat.

The drama continues to grip
our minds; the crowd larger;
finger on the trigger;

this assault forced upon us,
as I imagine greenbacks –
an orchard in me perhaps –

eloquent with each new card
a cue to meaning,
grappling with a youth's escape,

as hands proliferate like leaves
on a tree, this ruse of losing
one's money and succumbing

to art for art's sake:
I flutter in this make-believe,
clinging steadfastly to words!

ALEX'S STORY

He talks about Boris Lichstenfeldt, a poet
who gave up his job as an engineer
to shovel coals in Leningrad
so he could leave his mind free to write.

Next he says that I am now official:
the *poet laureate*; and if I were in
the Soviet Union, I'd have people coming
to me – many women – all asking

for my autograph. There, people read
books – about one hundred times more
than here, believe me, he emphasizes.
Ah, he has read Faulkner in Russia, and

a friend was translating him at the same time;
but Faulkner is stupid, he adds. *Why?*
His wife, also an emigre, who's been
living in New York since she was a child,

quickly says, "Sasha, do you remember the play
by the old Russian playwright? The one
that says whatever you don't understand
is stupid, eh?" They argue for a while.

He admits that lots of people in the Soviet Union
read Hemingway – even Boris Lichstenfeldt reads
him, though he's not absolutely sure about Faulkner.
His wife looks at him and make a strange face.

He's now glad to be in America, he says, where
he works with a computer firm. He finds flaws with

everything, and maybe his colleagues don't like that;
the programs they present to him have many faults;

but he has confidence in his boss. "Maybe, it's too
much politics here," he moans. His wife, with a
divorce yet to come, merely laughs at his effort
at quality control, American style!

(*Boston, August 1986*)

WANDERER

Being inside you, and it felt
      beautiful, as no other place,
really warm,

another galaxy in a world
      that whirs, kingdoms
coming to father other kingdoms;

      my breathing harder –
a mother, too, to those I've been
      accustomed to;

pretending to be loftier:
      murmuring hates, loves,
all to myself;

imagining so many worlds,
      streets without names,
entry points,

      other barricades, mucus, slime,
now falling apart at the limits,
      blood spurting

      or singing with joy, tunnels berating;
the man in white, a stethoscope,
      trembling;

      a shrill voice once again –
crying out because of who I am.
      Who? Travelling

across vagrant seas.

THE CALYPSONIAN

Say something political for him to hear –
      he will be *kaiso* at once, a *coonoomoonoo* man
ready to blare out in your ears
      like the gaffing poet with his dialect.

Next he will put two and two together
      and come up with verse, with rhymes distilled
under a palm tree, the waves always singing
      in the background, from every corner,

fanning the rhythms in your heart.
      He, once a Bad-John, gritting his teeth
in the gutter, now imagines love
      and eternal fame.

He will stand up and strum. Play on!
      Watch him stamp his feet, his body
swaying with island-rhythms; he, a man for all seasons,
      a real carnival holding sway.

But don't put him in a corner to breathe slowly
      by himself, or else another lyric
will come to his lips; he will quickly put you
      into rhyme, immortalize you

better than the gloomy poet would. His style
      is all that counts, his laughter
greater than waves rising, or wider than the expanse
      of an ocean. He will be like the vacation writer

filling you with sun and sparkling surprise.

LIVING WITHOUT PRETENCE

In Ottawa I am stuck
with being a Prime Minister
and Governor General.

I live out a protocol time,
lavishing praises, being
a Parliament breed, answering

questions about the universe
as I please. I make much ado about little,
consulting charts, figures.

I look around and pull a tie straight;
I stare at the camera,
remembering to smile,

not to be overly anxious.
I make faces when no one else is looking;
I am bored, but I am ready to shout

the rhetoric, to dazzle with wit.
It's a Parliament life all around,
walking along Bank and Rideau Streets.

I hardly read the newspapers any more;
I listen to the radio, watch TV:
these suffice.

What do I care
what Lynch or Gwnn says;
I make the country mine each time I step

across the Hill; I look around for anyone
suspicious, who might want to do harm,
or subvert.

I persist from day to day;
I remember to make my thoughts known,
muttering belief in the goodness of all men.

The Peace Tower clock chimes as I breathe harder –
A life drifting by in Ottawa, my future's limit.
Where else, world, do I go next?

TALKING AGAIN

for Antonino Mazza

Talking again of old songs,
of raging beasts
overcrowding the fields,

how we have come here
to live,
flinging the sun about

with centrifugal force,
blood coursing
through –

in whose body
is all this tremor
taking place?

More heaving
as I look back,
our lives falling apart

because we want to
live one thousand
years from now

from

BORN IN AMAZONIA (1995)

THE LEAP THAT TAKES
THE GROUND BY SURPRISE

Jaguar begins his run
as the spots fall invisibly
to the ground.

The forest heaves,
bark and pith in motion,
strides growing longer.

Thunder keeps pace
with lightning
in his footsteps;

more petals on grass,
rain next; a hoof beat
resounding

generations of the
animal-world. He knows
all things instinctively

with an ear-sound, a smell,
mirroring the sky
as he leaps high,

looking down next
at the fulsome world
with a massive growl.

JAGUAR DESCENDS TO THE DEAD

A seance
in the silence
of the forest

A tree stirs
Jaguar slowly
brushes its tail

Skin itches
Jaguar looks
for more signs

expecting
a dead grandmother
to appear

She's querulous
still
Jaguar humours her

with a growl
shows off his pelt
Grandmother collapses

Another death
as Jaguar waits
for her return

without fright

TWO THINGS FOUGHT

I gallop through barracks stripped of soldiers
and a foul army pursues me.
Pablo Neruda, "Dream Horse"

They held the day topsy-turvy;
they gathered dust and hurled it around
with a passion; they gritted teeth and swirled
eyes – contempt for the world-watchers.

One called upon the rodent-underground
to safeguard territory; the other hissed
the reptile's sense of genesis.
There was no retreat now.

They bruised each other in a frenzy;
they let out blood and chipped bone.
They grimaced and made the sun blink;
in the darkness they pulverized each other.

Men on a horse came, men from a dream,
spectral but real, overshadowing the pulp;
a hoof stood over, a body leaned across.
Life dragged along where the reptile and rodent

fought; in an amphitheatre, spectators' loss.

MYSTERY SONG

Something watched the two men
swimming to the mouth of the river.

Something understood the two men
moving with the current.

The men's faces were grim,
their teeth barricades against water,
a warning
sending a message
to the gums, eyes.

Something understood that the men
knew fear.
What else could they do?

Something merely stood back
and watched the men
being swallowed
by the leviathan
at the mouth of the river.

It wouldn't lend a hand,
didn't want to,
merely looked at others.

The men ended up nowhere,
into a further mouth,
opening into more mouths
without end.

QUEST

I keep looking out
for cities
on the dark side
of the moon

Same voice
or voicelessness;
I understand myself
less over the years

half-drunk in the sun
giving my only shirt
to cover the moon's
backside

like a justification
for love; so we continue
to embrace each other,
you, weeping,

the moon, old hen,
a rain-filled night
prodigal
with sameness.

THE BEAST

Hours after
     they left the dead one
on the brick-red road
     the other reptiles
     crawled out
and slowly dragged the beast
     back into the creek.

     They nursed him,
poured water out
     from their lungs,
     swallowed leaves
     and regurgitated them
onto his wounds.

Slowly the beast opened
     his eyes
and took in the others.
     He remembered death
and the noise
     of people around.

Next he wondered about water
     holding a mystery;
how life survived among
     his kind;
at once he knew prehistory,

registering it with a splash
     which made all things
wonder where from
     they actually came.

LIFE AMONG THEM

Tonight the old stars gather around
without the wish to take anyone by surprise.

It's the same all over again.

The river continues its mild stretch.

I answer questions about a life
I know little about.

Old friends help me make a beginning.

I make a promise to the village.

I share out my blood.

How long I will keep my promise
I'm not sure.

The moon silently passes by
like a familiar mute.

All is not well; this I know.

I turn away in febrile forgetfulness.

JIM JONES REVISITED

I.

Hands upraised; an ant
walking about
in a circle;
        a jaguar snarls,
teeth bared
        in Dadanawa, Rupununi.

I am watchful,
waiting, as the door
        slowly opens;
leaves are spread out
        as in a barricade.
I look out, preaching
        with my hands tied
behind my back,
        seated on a chair:
a jaguar's face, eyes
solid as moons.

        I establish foundations,
a garden universe,
        an ocelot time
with macaw/tapir/agouti/ant-
        eater/sloth.
A hand before my eyes,
I walk like Daniel
into the lion's den. Talk
        of love, echoes
everywhere, stalking
        my own shadow.

My fulsome paradise:
I plough the ground, reaping yams
plantains, cassava;
drink piawiri – a drunk
Arawak, swallowing
the stars whole, breathing
in the mountains, belching
the sea – Borges' blue tiger,
footprints indelible on sand.

II.

Here it is
a sucrose time without
        slave rebellion,
twenty million stemming the tides;
        the Middle Passage's below deck,
hands and feet tied,
        ringing out
        hallelujahs!

        Welcome to the clarion call,
high heaven, low earth,
        the bloated sun in my midst,
a fetid moon dripping blood,
        pellets of rain.

        Give me a virgin,
to do with as I please:
        the upheaval of flesh,
teeth biting in,
        drinking you raw, this
benediction uttered,
        a song of praise,
        and anointing.

More corn/sugar cane/bananas
        and spirited rum in the dark:
I drink and drink, and talk loudest
        of all men's love,
ransoming the sun,
        the thickets weeded out, but mosquitoes
yet palpable.
        Such socialist semblance –
ah, shun the evil deed!

Keep girding thy loins, while I still nightly
        roam: Sarah for me, Sam
        next; Sandra, Elizabeth too –
I a hail fellow, not easily well met.
        Whiplash rhapsody:
these tremors of love
and intermittent forgiveness.

III.

        A sudden storm,
raindrops like pellets sinking in
        loam and clay, the hinterland
soil fertile – as I am stark and bare,
        my utopia crumbling. America
resounds: a senator smooths his lapels,
        frowning at the evidence: case history
after case history unfolds in California.

God's law and human covenant;
        it's noisier. Prostrate now
I drink with ease,
        satiety about to do for me.
Let this be a warning to your kind.
        Our kind will take the world by storm;
hereafter, another Babel.

Shun the Moscovite
        reciting hosannas
from a donkey's back! Magdalene, my sweet,
        hear my voice, swallow hard. Sweet blood
        of Jesus! Do this, do that – a gun
at my side. Helicopter's blades
beat! Now ask the right questions.
        What bodies are hidden? On what video screen
do you wish to display
the scorch of the tropical heat,
the virulence of man's deed?

        No need to entertain your kind, especially
        men who write. Believe me,
the flock's all the same. Or do you think
        I am insane?
Not the sun's splendour
        in a jaguar's paradise, this snatching
of a child, head in first...

IV.

I breathe heavily, longing for the coast
as death invades the jungle,
a loudspeaker's breath left in me.
Hear ye, hear ye!

Do you drown?
Are you the hangman upside down?
Children, speak loudest, blessed all!
Shun the outsiders, keep us forever one...

Take count, how many bodies lie bloated
in the sun? Am I with you?

Do I drink the bitter pill of insanity?
Flesh breeds flesh. The colours darkly etch.

The hinterland's a darkish-red,
sunset under an umbrella sky,
the leaves coming down like a tarpaulin,
covering the bewildered earth...

Who will finally listen? Who will watch?
Who cringe in the distance?
My benediction's hereafter –
hymn to a clown!

REHEARSAL

"Language the chameleon seeks to explain
the chameleon reality." A.I.

Old father tongue sticking out
over the fenced yard,
scampering out from the coop,
the reptilian self
breaking out without a warning,

changeable again, across the barrier
scattering feathers,
a life gone rampant
in dreams, the insane among us presenting
emblems from the scuttled sea;

all talk, old words, dropping scales
the dung of reality; moonshape
pitching stars from the tips
of my fingers, blood oozing at the thighs,
wetting the ground to form our roots.

WORDS & LEGACY

My father's life is alchemy
he tightens a fist at the wind
he plunges himself with an anger

into the night. He berates all-comers
with a dagger-kill. He listens
to the howling wind presaging his death

I wake up from a dream after the first cockcrow
I remember how folklore is vivid
in nightmares

how in frenzy a father's words
become the thin edge of a blade
he goes on living from day to day

making the sun blink

QUETZALCOATL, PLUMED SERPENT

I.

When the gods become more human
life takes a turn for the worse.

He began by changing things around;
it was no longer necessary to offer
the human heart as sacrifice.
Butterflies, frogs, crickets –
a myriad of different things
were just as good.

They began to think he was weak,
that perhaps he was addled,
he knew nothing of scorpions
in other men's minds, or of solid gold
bars emblazoning the sky.

II.

Montezuma kept waiting;
he heard of their coming;
he thought of the plumed serpent at once
whose return was always on his mind;
he waited with an open heart,
little anxious as Cortez stepped closer.

They wore helmets of steel,
sailing down the river to Tenochtitlan;
they brandished swords;
and Montezuma prayed for further vision
to keep his heart still warm,

wondering if the plumed one was coming
in strong anger to surprise them
under the Inca sun

III.

At his dying, he remembered
he would eat his own heart out
for a sacrifice; and with scaly eyes
he realized how the ground-dust swirled
under his feet with the others' presence.

FULL-FLEDGED

I continue
to dream about the poem
that is full of surprises

a poem born from
alligators' eggs
a hybrid poem
that takes images
from nightmares

a chimera poem
dog-face poem
cat's paw poem

a poem that will kill
once it is read
a miraculous poem
that will make its listeners
contort with pain
burn their insides
starting with
the middle ear
make people gyrate
and dance

a poem at the gate
barking loudly
seizing a whole amphitheatre

catapulting everyone
to their death.

A BORROWED HEAD

It understood the essence of things;
it fought against arrant display
in lawn and park, against other faces
that mocked and jeered;

it realized that there were things
it shouldn't do. It heaved with false breath,
a fulsome ear; it breathed to fill lungs like an udder;
it squirted from the tip of its tongue,
coiled like a horn without elegance.

It bellowed with rage as the evening grew dark;
other faces looked on,
eyes squinting in an angle of light,
warning that there's something else in life,
at the heart of all things, breathing.

But only when alone did it begin
to realize how little it understood
the one head in which it had lived all along;
will now remind itself that a head
borrowed will live seventy years
or less before turning to mould, then
disintegrate like any number
of rancid things, and finally become
sun and soil – elemental again –
the one thing it was
meant to be
from the very beginning.

BRAMALEA, NOT A DIRGE

I ask my brother:
When our father dies
        should we go to his funeral?

I haven't been back in ten years;
my father is somewhere close to anonymity,
his other children having grown up –
        many of whom I hardly know.

Back there they talk
about me from time to time;
here my brother notes how his kids
        hang out at the Bramalea city centre.

Once a radical of sorts, my brother watches
his son distributing the right wing *Toronto Sun*
at weekends, listens to Madonna
        on a disc vibrating loudly.

I urge my brother to take instant action.
Laughter! And I imagine my father
        becoming greyer.

As if not thinking, I make a promise
to pay the costs
of my father's funeral –
when that time comes –
        to everyone's utter surprise.

VISAGE

This onslaught
of rain

thunderclapping
the heart

out of my body
the visage

long & grey
the martyr sun

beating its chest
flowers bursting out

from the ribcage
of the moon

from

DISCUSSING COLUMBUS (1997)

ADRIFT

You knew the world, miraculously,
like an egg on your palm, studying its shape,
geodesic in a way...

Italy's or Spain's shores going farther away,
our Europe's distance, an entire ocean throbbing
in the sun's eye – each wave an eyebrow;

beginnings all over again; other places, a twig's
foreshadowing, a caravel of lost time,
twirling fingers, all hands on deck.

This thrashing of waves all around,
the momentum of a fish flying suddenly,
or a miracle of trinity-peaked mountains.

Further images of men with heads between their
shoulders, beasts or gods; my Arawak's or Carib's face
of fear – welcoming, mirageous again.

The ocean rolling back like a giant carpet,
and mindful of you, lifted up,
pushing from behind a huge boulder,

feet firmly planted
on new soil, this groundless earth,
looking up at a contemptuous sky.

AND YOU...

And you, I know, you, with buttressed roots;
other trees, the ocean rising;

people from far-off places, crouching;
I have walked with the jaguar –

I keep coming down
on lianas from taller trees,

foam-like, blood pouring out,
the splash of other days...

And I am at the bottom
of a large blue sea with Borges –

the moon springing up,
a tarpaulin of clouds, as you

raise your hands, armpits, all;
there's hope and fear, the beast

with the child in its mouth at the crest
of a wave... screaming

And is no more!

TO AN ISLAND

Hold me to an island,
hold me still, but keep me tied to other places:
valleys, whole rivers,
        the streets continually
appearing in dreams.

I am once more at it, mouth agape,
        beginning anew –
        other places that keep the imagination
at a standstill.

Adventure at the crossroads at odd hours
        of the night –
like floating cigarette packets
        in one's childhood;
a river thrashing in moonlight.

Now my confederation of lost loves,
ways of asking mountains
to account for their aloofness.
The sun has held dominion
for too long.

I touch soft ground, cry out with a fierce pain,
        mightily shrill,
still holding myself to an island, trees, groves,
rivers meandering, again darkwatered,
        this Demerara or Orinoco –
the tongue expressing itself in silence

like a burden of cloth or patchwork,
feet firmly planted, the ground still topsy-turvy –
        the sky merely standstill.

DISCUSSING COLUMBUS
"All the peoples of the world are human"
(Batholome de las Casas)

I talk in tongues of newness,
I fulfil a rage without disdain;
I am the voice within, I cringe,
coming to an understanding
of who I am, where I am going next;
this Columbus in me, smashing the waves
into smithereens with bare hands.

Next, making much ado about Behring Straits,
talking myself hoarse at the zenith
of a totem pole, or grimacing at the bear
in the sky, I am a shaman at ease
discussing treaties with the RCMP,
a constitutional accord, this bleeding self's disdain,
being partridge and beaver,
or all of spruce and jackpine.

Still making memory out of nothing,
collecting cambium and spitting it out
at the face of the Great Spirit,
the sky golden, a rainbow's own crossing,
the sunset falling under,
this cave, again a sudden divide,
I linger and laugh at other boundaries
which I do not understand...

I live with the centuries' folds of skin,
other emblems like shale, rock, an entire shield –
my canoe's surfacing at the heart of a lake;
and the partridge yet hops about in the dark,
the sun's pitch-blackness
across this Turtle Island.

Drink in me, I entangle and enmesh
all the regions as one, bracing myself
with a tightrope as more waves come in,
the ships' own somersault,
the ground breaking at the horizon,
the sails' language, which I repeat or memorize
on a deserted but peopled land!

HALLOWEEN AT THE GOVERNOR GENERAL'S

I am disguised;
I am not myself.

I am common folk,
excited by the privilege

of being here, of mixing
with the rich –

even as I overhear
one MP and his coterie

wondering why So-and-So
are here; who invited them;

with a different government
it might be otherwise;

and one long-standing member
showing his manners,

suddenly bursts into song
about the plight of the people

of Grenada
(pronounced *G-r-a-n-a-d-a*)

a hundred times over –
like a bullfrog croaking

in the stillness across
a stygian Rockliffe night

rife with monsters and demons
swarming all over.

EVOLUTION SONG

I have evolved
from sugar cane
(so goes the hoary
Indian myth)

I sprout leaves
in the sun
unleashing
blades in the wind

arrows pointing upward
as I am tropical
to the bone,

tramping on
squelchy ground
after the heavy rain

whacking
at the seasons
with machete haste

my sucrose memory
reeks through
molasses time

PASSAGES TO INDIA
(or Getting to Know Tigers Better)

Rukmin, one of the cubs,
had several tastes of Mrs. Walker
in accidental bites and scratches,
but showed no tendency to develop
a taste for human flesh.

While Mrs. Walker agrees that tiger cubs
cannot resist attacking
a bending or squatting
human being – "I have experienced
numerous attacks of this kind,"
she says – she certainly

wouldn't be willing
to offer herself for an experiment
of this kind with a full-grown tiger.
The above is borne out
by reports of tigers attacking
people bent over while gathering

wood or grass, or simply squatting.
The victims naturally scream or struggle;
then the true natural instinct
of the tigers to what they bite
is incited!

Mrs. Walker avers, "Once a person
is dead, he's just meat and fair game
for dinner; the law of the jungle
allows little sentiment, really..."

TELLING YOU

I.

This is not to tell you
that I pretend to be Paz, Rabassa, or Llosa,

or that I am still anxious to know who you are –
you who had all the answers, beyond language

in Canada that summer, the whir of conversation,
accents, our being on familiar ground.

A decade later, the walls of the building
are all I am left with, thinking of the films

we watched, image after image, returning
like home-grown truths. Beaches. Cancun.

The ruins, too, still lapping. Maybe you're
settled down now with an *esposa* and *niños*.

II.

Another cold night in Ottawa's Island Park Drive,
here where Canada's first terrorist killing occurred

(the Turkish Ambassador being shot – and I am
neither Armenian nor immune, being spoiled

by the middle class). At a reception, you *muchacha*,
offered another *marguerita* – and are you really

Spanish? What better half do you portray?
– your sensitive mouth, face like the young girls

in the village I grew up in. You, Mexicana really?
I've decided to wait for the Cultural Attaché

to return after month's end since I am
selfishly after a poetry reading.

Oh how I dreamt of the dark-haired Peruvian woman,
now settled here, who is divorced but stable.

Desire is still all. Ah, the Mexican Ambassador
is in Montreal tonight, you say, cringing a little

because of the questions I ask. His wife is pleasant,
more Spanish than Mexican; she holds up a one-year old

child; her other is twelve years apart, she says,
and smiles; and I am still travelling with you,

being Garcia, Borges, and Fuentes –
and Guillen and Neruda at the heart of a sacrifice,

giving the best part of myself –
to be close to Montezuma.

THE HIDDEN SUN

On dry land, this dance,
this lifting the body in the air
like a somersault;
and, wind in the stomach,
aching with ruptures.

The colours break out on slopes,
other distances, valleys;
I am rolling within, body
crumbling like falling snow.

Here are the boundaries,
as I sustain myself.
It is further green,
the landscape all ours.

And taking you home this night
I ring out the cry.
Again hard steps, ground
sucking me in.
Mud. Swamp.

Our foreign beginnings.

FULL MOON

Sarah belly gaan fo' swell up
an' she head bend down

she soul ready fo' pick up fire
she hand in she mout'

she teeth sharp-sharp like razor
tho' she eye dull like senna

wait now fo' hear wha' she go say
how she want this thing fo' go away

heh-heh, you see he a come, starboy-like
you see he a go away, gangster-like

he brazen all the way –
Sarah now eager fo' throw away she belly

imagining she child down an alleyway –
wait fo' hear what she go say now

how she na really want
this thing fo' go away!

LETTER TO DEREK WALCOTT
(for Jack Healy)

This January night is bitterly cold,
but I have made a special effort to be here
to hear you fashion a tale once more
of Mighty Spoiler returning from the dead
and watching over our islands;
in you the Tiresias-eye,
perhaps "still poisoned by the blood of both",
or this language you still love so much.

Here, distantly recalling the region's calypso
or carnival, or thinking of my own growing up
with the affectation of words,
my dreams made more solid from afar;
here where there are also falsifiers
as we continue this travesty of selves,
or try reshaping myth with Cutteridge's
cow jumping over the moon
at odd moments in the coldest winter
as much as in warmer weather,
despite Time's slavery and indenture.

Now your first time in this capital city –
place of embassies, bureaucracy – here with
its Third World Players and my own *Shapely Fire*
on a changing Canadian landscape –
our continuing to be proud of high art;
and Spoiler is palpably here, too,
with the semblance of royalty; your words
etched among professors and graduate
students of Commonwealth Literature,

215

evoking more than star-apple kingdoms
in a green night
       echoing monkey mountain or jungle
– take your pick.

Yes, tired as you seem now – your being
away from Brodsky's Boston,
after reading three nights
in a row, after Toronto, and your talking
to the Indian girls from Guyana (or Trinidad?),
despite your quarrel with "V.S. Nightfall";
you tell me of Sangster, or better still
express greetings to Hosein.
      Maybe you are
too anxious to reveal much else,
relaxed as you are with Gordon, Stanford,
and Walters – all Players – their saying how glad
they are to meet you (again); and it's as if
they're truly surprised by your measured tones;
your former shyness or the dialect
that's always best – though not the accustomed
tones of "after the hot-gospeller...."
Still pulsating with language,
your own fires bright here on the Carleton
University campus – your tropics in our winter –
applause is never too much.

(January 20, 1989)

AQUEDUCT

From where we stand,
continuation of rivers, forests,
rhododendron boughs, and the hopes
we fashion: new cities, courtyards –
ourselves like pillars of salt –
redrawing the boundaries...

*

Far-off cries: ethnics crossing,
shiploads at a time – Romanesque too –
others pillaging the sluiced terrain,
fish at the end of the line;
this hook of ancestry (if you must know),
catchment or making amends...

*

We stretch out with skin,
baffled by the tides, the expression
one of myriad streams,
history's suspended memory,
mutterings of custom, heritage, other
languages we call our own, and are not really...

*

Then disaster with sage brush, acacia;
water hyacinths at the edge of a storm;
other pathways: still words without meaning
as we look out for laws, canon, erecting
monuments, and not recognizing our own
in this blood and meshed skin. Here where
the sun's brightest...

*

So we crown ourselves, crashing
against the ocean all over again;
thighs splayed out – all our longings
or desires; so we acknowledge or accept
fates more glorious than our own
in this North, coming
to a vague understanding
of who we are not.

HEMINGWAY

With you, I sip one *mojito* after another.
    I too write my name on the wall
of this restaurant, eating hot Spanish rice
    and enjoying it as never before.

With you, at the Havana Libre (the former Hilton),
    I listen to the plump, light-skinned
woman operating the elevator,
    who hasn't yet left for Miami,

who now asks for American dollars.
    With you, I walk the streets this night
watching healthy young Cubans saunter about
    by the seawalls, hand in hand, much in love;

and I enter the well-lit narrow streets
    close to the harbour, where I am accosted
by two seductive-looking girls
    who explain their need for clothes

and other amenities (*trienta dolares,*
    por favor!). With you too, I drink in the spectacle
of *La Tropicana* and later reminisce
    over Afro-Cubano rhythms, debating workers' rights

to such incentives in a proletariat state –
    all eloquence to a revolution; here where
I breathe fully of the old Spanish town
    and linger by La Universidad de Habana,

entering a hall uninvited, where for the first time
    I see posters of Castro outdo those of Marti,
and as I am about to leave (you never really did,
    Hemingway), I wonder about Batista's island-paradise,

transformed; maybe I too belong here: your
     marlin's sea reaches up to me in the sun's sweep
on this bone of island –
     as my blood is also on the rise.

ANOTHER PLACE

for Ken Ramchand

Along the North and South Ranges,
or looking back from Tobago,

I take for granted your aloofness,
with trees bending to the lip of the sea.

All journeys have their sources, I say,
what we acknowledge and will soon forget:

a hummingbird twittering loudly,
or a Carib offering a blood sacrifice

to an ancient god at La Brea;
the Chaguanas sun on a Caroni swamp,

fronds wavering because of what the eyes
cannot see from the distant white North.

Indeed, let us remain in one place
for more than a lifetime, you declare.

Debris will never overtake us
as we come to regard weather as landscape.

The mountains start withering or shrinking
at the speed of light in the sunset,

and I bid you farewell with arabesques
of memory that will never fade –

because of the ways of the ocean,
the wind stronger without the usual

hurricane; the sun still going down...
to the bottom of a deeper sea.

DRIVING WITH FRED D'AGUIAR TO MIAMI BEACH
(for D.D.)

Taking off almost helicopter fashion
like a strange memory – I fathom
space or time with self doubt, feeling
haywire in the strong wind in the back seat
of Fred's topless car.

Debbie's hair flustered,
blown about, I hold onto my glasses,
and Fred turns, looking back at me,
not wanting my glasses to be hurled away, he says;
in the breathtaking speed of space
I imagine overcoming great distances,
or quietly wonder where is actually home.

Going across the giant causeway,
taking in the Miami skyline, spectacular
at night, as the car travels faster
we recall the Canadian hurdler-sprinter
Mark McCoy – Fred has his good looks,
but lacks the hurricane strides –
and joke of the Guyanese's natural burst of speed.

Like a wind-surfer, I am
overwhelmed, or simply being
too excited on Miami Beach, still fathoming
space, or determining where I must
continue to dream about another place –

boundaries – reminiscences of London
or Amherst, even longing to be elsewhere
at special moments – evanescent over time
because of what I have always cherished
and will always remember best
in days to come,
        or gone by.

CAPILANO SUSPENSION BRIDGE

I am shaking at the edge;
the universe is coming
to ruin;
I am talking myself hoarse.

Let the river suspend
all motion –
I will continue to talk to myself
before the twin-peaked mountains;

I will leap against the tides with salmon
and other furies;
I continue to hover and teeter at the edge;
I will cling further,

Tarzan-like if I must,
challenging other worlds.
I am here to stay,
a liana-memory, fazed

in the heat, heart once more
awry. The colours take on
fury, vermilion, russet,
still chameolonic.

I am crepuscular
one last time at the crest,
drifting with a remnant
cloud, swinging at the horizon,

and the water below
is giddy with the imprint
of lions' feet,
the ground swirling;

and two sisters we are,
more than siblings –
thrashing in the ecstasy,
plunging down,

myriad-faced,
Haida still in me!

NEW POEMS

FOR A STUDENT AT THE DELHI COLLEGE
OF ARTS AND COMMERCE

Who does he think he is? He comes here and talks of
places: the Caribbean and South America where he was born,
yet believing all worlds far apart.
      I am keen on Pink Floyd,
and other British and American rock stars

come to mind. I know my place –
and all ways of crossing an ocean
in a dhow – and it's not just tea or poverty, or my going
      beyond the TV image or imagining a future
more than a bearded astrologer ever could,
      or listening to a harmonium's mournful wail,
or the sitar's – the old man hunched in a corner
      in a sidewalk in Delhi. Listen well.

My poverty, your richness. My caste system, too.
      Dare I tell how Brahminic days are coming to an end –
 the Dalits making loud noises as Parliament
      echoes with boasts, or mere flattery –
and there's the 60 million tribespeople somewhere in the mountains;
and do you know the Himalayas are still growing?
      I've longed to travel, recreating Marco Polo,
not just John Cabot heading for Newfoundland;
      and the *Titanic* moving towards an iceberg
is more than magic realism with a rock speaking
      from the crevices. Sirens, if you must know!

History of the East India Company in Calcutta or a
      Viceroy in Shimla avoiding the Delhi summer heat,
(while Gandhi traipsed around the country with religious fervour
      despite imminent partition); or nuclear-bomb
hysteria – Kashmir yet making strides; or Pakistan's

military-government's threat: tell me of that too,
     instead of Blackbeard in the seductive Caribbean.

Now a rock n' roll revolution is everywhere, I hear –
my being an upstart – and it's my turn to bring you other truths
despite Kipling and his unbelievable Mowgli,
     or the jewel-in-the-crown test once again –
still more than music of the spheres
      while you try to sustain a tryst with destiny
because Nehru and other Congress Party stalwarts
     faced greater odds than I could ever imagine...
as I come to grips with your Canadian ways –
     an exchange of our common heritage really.

FOR CLAIRE

The poem keeps calling her back, it doesn't want her to leave
for places afar, or just close up. It's the Irish Sea too
as it makes waves to her, pretends to be a Sirens' song
far back in time – a memory of beginnings,
not just an ending; indeed it calls out to her louder
because of journeys yet to be undertaken.

The poem goes to Cloughey Beach with this flashback:
picking up shells with her, embracing her as the sea air
becomes a sudden gust; indeed, the poem wants to go further,
to those moments in her childhood, imagining her
as never seen, the tide ebbing or quickly rising
as she looks from a window because of what's ahead.

The poem has water in its eyes as it takes her in fully,
as sea gulls skirt above, swerving in midair as the tide rises,
and what's seen on the horizon seems to retreat.
It's never the same again as the poem pretends to understand
and goes with her again to Belfast, if not Dublin, all now akin
to ancient quarrels with Gaelic voices loudest.

The poem's intention's to be always with her,
beckoning to her, with her father distantly smiling, or just
walking with her from Trinity College, then to Dun Laoghaire
and Glengarry. Houses look back too as the poem takes
more deliberate steps, accompanying her with a rhythm
all its own and wondering how to make amends.

GIRL ON THE DUN LAOGHAIRE PIER

The ships move out, and even from long ago
time does not reveal secrets of where
they travelled. Silent waters
remain while you consider your father's ways,
his hand in yours. He's in spaces distant
from your own, with an innocence of the spirit,
a timelessness in this Dublin most of all.

More ships keep coming in, or leaving,
your father thinking, going deeper into himself;
and you, now looking back, maybe wishing
you knew him more, knew what indeed
he kept imagining – memory of loss, with
waves washing, or the ships at anchor and
the sailors' own brooding spell. All you
now bring to bear is because of
what's beyond, still walking hand in hand
with him on Dun Laoghaire pier.

Nothing ever truly disappears, is never lost.
The poem brings it back: familiar waters,
real places, your father most of all: this faith
or tenderness in him, being more than instinct
or intuition, the tremor of bones, the blood
vessels' own. As waves keep beating
you breathe harder, because of the Troubles,
or just the Irish Sea making new promises
to those in distant shores, in Canada.

This pulses in you as he comes yet closer,
while you write your own verse, contemplating
waves on the horizon moving farther out,
or more distantly still, as if from another shore–
this timelessness of things occurring.

BLACK FACES

You can paint
in any colour
you like,
said the
old lady
to Conan,
the five-year-old
boy in the Dublin
train going
to Belfast.

He showed
his picture
book around,
with black faces only.
I turned
to the old
lady
and muttered
that I could
have been born
in Dublin too,

my being here
all my life.
My wife smiled –
being coy – her way –
Irish-born herself.

And my daughter,
an artist too,
made eye contact
with the boy –
a face of colour,

merely...
as Conan
lifted his book
to hide his smile —
distances between us,
now with shapes only.

(Aug. 9, 2003)

THE CRUSADER

I.

He might have hefted a sword,
brandished it, lopped heads off,

hurled himself as his horse
reared on its hind legs – more than

Picasso's in his *Guernica* ever did –
because of religious faith, you see.

He berated other worlds, heathens all,
this man buried in St. Michan's Church

in Dublin City – a mummy, 800-years old,
as I contemplate and sniff the limestone air.

II.

The church's guide, without blarney,
but with no less enthusiasm, invites me

to touch the hand of this Crusader –
to bring me luck, unbeliever as I may be.

It's just superstition, I think,
through the ages I have imagined, but

it's what keeps driving us with blood
beating in the veins, because of what might

have been in times past with other faiths,
rising up with an inhalation of the chest:

boundaries we carry in us, or with us
because of stronger beliefs than in me.

III.

Yet I still contemplate faith, being a Moor
or a Mogul – more than Yeats ever did,

despite a Second Coming – or think of
wars once more being fought at will –

this clash of civilizations again –
as I hurry out of the crypt, sniffing

the air because the dead have ways
of coming after us with yet more wars,

conjuring up my being a crusader
of sorts and murmuring regret,

thinking of this one here who will
remain lifeless for long ages to come.

Superstitious I may be, I reclaim
what's lost – or brace up for ill-luck.

SPACES

We never talked, we withstood words,
we let silence take over,
we narrowed the corners, reached a cul-de-sac.

We parlayed with more vociferous appeals
because language knows its limits.
The vowels and consonants hissed

back at me, the days ending
without a meeting place.
Here in the tunnel where it's dark

we face each other, just berating
the self in silence, chewing words –
not unlike chomping at the bit –

this throbbing of the heart,
and saying I love you
while we are far apart;

and there's moments
of relapse, and nothing
to say any more

save for the memory
of who we are,
from a far distance

if only still close-up.

ALEXANDER HAMILTON
(after Sanskrit)

I was dogged, determined
about India, you see;
I wanted to know everything
there is to know, every jot of it.

Sanskrit most of all;
and who were the Aryans,
Dravidians in the south:
dark or fair skinned?

It's what an Englishman
will tell you, maybe not
with your expected tone,
or sense of Empire, the Raj no less.

Language or just a constellation,
like stars without the sense
of otherworldliness, is all I've thought
about in Delhi or Benares.

To France I came next, place still
at the heart of things, continent
on the horizon without astrological signs
I conjure up, or it's what's left behind.

Now it's the East again, you better believe,
this virtue of knowing how things
turned exotic, what words shaped
origins, as they still affect us

more than the Vedas ever did –
holy books with the gods always having their way,
as a determined poet like Kalidas
of Shakuntala fame reflected.

How I yearned to be back in England,
but being a prisoner in France,
I bargained for my freedom –
cataloguing books in a Paris library.

Oh, books of the Orient, being written
down before I could sail again,
or learn what's in store for us...
the stars being like nowhere else.

WHAT THEY SING ABOUT IN FOREIGN PLACES

El Dorado – it's because of the one who came and searched
for pitch to caulk his leaky vessels – now, do you want to come
with me, as we return there, taking one step at a time,
with memory overshadowing everything else? How men
continue to sing the one song that makes life worthwhile!

How we relive what happened long ago!
You'll see, in Brazil or somewhere else,
a place John Donne might have long considered,
with visions of the hinterland – this new consciousness,
a city of gold – or just the reshaping of what's in
the imagination, the image of a town in a far-off land.

Let the hoary men in Manaus come closer –
all in the Amazon – if it's just to hear them sing louder,
and inhale deeply because of the life everyone keeps
living through the ages, as men yet long for gold.
Oh, this El Dorado again: the king Manoa keeps bathing
in gold dust in shadowy places. Light flickers
and we cover our eyes and listen to words we've come
to know so well, or just echoes as Raleigh's
History of the World keeps being written in the tower –
what I remember longest and will tell once more about.

AMAZONIA

(for Miguel Neneve,
University of Rondonia)

We discussed how Caribbean
writers only look north,
and how maybe I'm unique
among them (I want to believe)
because of my interest
in all of South America.

Indeed, when you came to my home
in Ottawa, we ate
barbecued capybara,
and for starters swallowed
anaconda's eggs whole –
        you better believe it –
and drank Irish beer,
Guinness and Smithwick's
(I'd just returned from Dublin, you see,
spent time at the Writers' Museum
with Yeats and Joyce,
Behan and Beckett).

You told me of the time
when you wanted to come
to Georgetown from Brazil,
to the university, and travelled
to Boa Vista on the border,
and ended up in Lethem
where you planned to board
        a plane...

    But somehow
a cow had hit the plane
and the trip was cancelled,

and with another woman,
with your scholar's ways,
you travelled to Venezuela instead
to continue your work: this interest
in poetry – mine, if only for a while,
because I'd been *born in Amazonia*.

Now you snap a picture of
my daughter, with my wife
looking on; and Pilar from Spain,
keen on Margaret Atwood,
noted our different ways
in the one place I call home –
far more than Canadian Studies,
now that we're indeed here.
  (Aug. 18, 2003)

THE TABLA PLAYER

All life is rhythm
Ustad Alla Rakha

I played the drum
alone, on the kitchen table,
imagining a far place, my knuckles
cracking on stiff board,
      fingers and wrist movements –

a far continent really,
as I began tracing the Ganges,
      moving by train
from Madras in the south,
      all the way up
north to Shimla
      in the Himalayas –

the tabla player I was meant to be,
from the very beginning –
      though little did I know,
being born in South America,
      with the Orinoco
and other rivers close by –

as I kept on playing,
      crossing new terrain,
like a new hemisphere,
      recalling Hemant Kumar,
the famed playback singer
      who came to our village
with his troupe of musicians,
      the tabla drummers and sitar men,
now active in my imagination.

Memory, indeed, is
     all with me in Canada,
as I recall the desire to be best
     on stage in Bombay or Calcutta –
still pretending to play the tabla –
     my knuckles grown harder;

and it's because of where I was born,
     as my mother
wonders what I've left behind:
     the sounds she yet hears,
and claps her hands
     before a silent stage.

POST-CANNIBALISM
(for Douglas Kerr)

Up your
arse,
Robinson Crusoe.

It's not just
pidgin talk,
but words
encoded.

You make
an 'authentic' pilgrim's
progress –

on an (un)deserted
island.
Dammit Crusoe,
the Cross you carry

is your burden,
salvation being always
at hand for you –

but never me.
I piss on your head,
because of the name
I carry; oh, what a name –

Man Friday –
unlike Solomon Gundy
born on a Monday,

christened on Tuesday.
Cannibal I may be
but this bread I break
with you

is hardly flesh.
What I wish to devour
is sacramental time,

because of the life we live
far from home,
in foreign territory –
Empire being all –

with meaning more solid
than I care to think about,
all things being signified.

BREAKING FREE

He rode his horse
pistons beating,
his Pegasus body
       flapping wings.

Clouds somersault,
clods of earth
      in the air,
as he gallops faster

in the familiar sun
with girth & mane,
   lightning & thunder,
into greater space.

Further strides in my midst,
  as topsoil grows harder,
      binocular eyes
forming at the track's end.

Slowly he comes to a realization,
  of who he is.
      Like a noiseless death,
the reins he holds tighter,

heaving in the wind,
  the horizon before him,
     as the animal
suddenly snorts louder.

Foam at the mouth,
  the horse is folded down
     in the stabled dark;
now against sun & sky

reflecting the sea's glare,
   as the animal stares
      farther ahead,
still open-eyed.

INDEX OF FIRST LINES

REVIEWS OF CYRIL DABYDEEN'S WORK

"Movements, rhythms, sensations, emotions and images from the Caribbean, from South America, and from Canada enliven his poetry. The book (*Coastland*) bristles with energy and bursts with life... a lively and colourful book."
John Robert Colombo, *The Ottawa Citizen*

"...his ability to speak from both Caribbean and Canadian contexts gives his work much of its power."
Bronwen Wallace, *The Ottawa Citizen*

"In the tradition of Pablo Neruda and Nicolas Guillen, Dabydeen expresses strong sympathies for the poor and a feeling for the hard ironies of existence..." **Patricia Morley,** *The Ottawa Journal*

"...a gifted Canadian poet." *The Toronto Star*

"Dabydeen's poems have Stravinsky's rhythms." *The Ottawa Citizen*

"I enjoyed your poems....They are rich, and shot through with an incongruous quality that is the work of outstanding art."
Roy Heath, novelist (UK)

"It is a wonderful thing for a reader to hear someone's voice in the truest sense – and that voice is present in your poems – and in the prose." **Robert Sward (poet, San Francisco)**

Dabydeen poems are "diamond-sharp, polished with expert skill ...an exciting craftsman!" *The Canadian Author and Bookman*

"Cyril Dabydeen has carved out a special audience over the years... His work reflects a unique sense of history and consciousness, making him distinctive. Writing always with passion and honesty, he blends both an outsider and insider perspective of Canada in a compelling vision." **Joy Kogawa** (novelist, poet)

ABOUT THE AUTHOR

Cyril Dabydeen was born in the Canje, Guyana, in 1945. His father was a marginal cattle farmer, his mother a seamstress. He grew up with his grandmother and an extended family of aunt, nieces, nephews. His grandfather, a driver on the Rose Hall sugar estate, died when Cyril Dabydeen was very young, and the family survived through running a small-scale cakeshop.

When he left school at sixteen, he worked as a pupil teacher at the St Patrick's Anglican School between 1961-70. Like most young Indo-Guyanese of his generation and background he was an active supporter of Cheddi Jagan's Marxist PPP, and his politics remain true to those radical ideals. He began writing in this period, winning the Sandbach Parker Gold Medal for poetry in 1964; his first pamphlet of poems, *Poems in Recession*, was published in 1972.

In the early 1970s he left Guyana for Canada to obtain higher education, and he obtained a BA (First class Hons) at Lakehead University, an MA and an MBA at Queens University. From the late 1970s, he wrote and published with energy, rapidly establishing a reputation as an important new poet in both Canada and the Caribbean.

During the 1970s, he was also writing short stories, and a first collection *Still Close to the Island* was published in 1980, followed by *To Monkey Jungle* in 1988. His first novels, published by Peepal Tree, *Dark Swirl* and *The Wizard Swami* came out in 1989. Since then there has been a further collection of short stories, *Berbice Crossing* (1996).

More recently he has published in Canada *Jogging in Havana*, *Black Jesus and Other Stories* (1997), *My Brahmin Days and other Stories* (2000), *Drums of My Flesh* (2005), *Play A Song Somebody: New and Selected Stories* (2005), *Uncharted Heart* (2008), *Unanimous Night* (2009).

The Wizard Swami, 0-948833-19-X, £6.99

When Devan, the awkward boy from Providence Village, finds his vocation as a teacher of Hinduism to the rural Indians of the Corentyne Coast of Guyana, his life and his troubles begin. In this richly comic novel, Cyril Dabydeen creates a vibrant picture of the Guyanese Hindu community struggling for a place in what is for Devan a confusingly multi-racial country. When Devan leaves his village and his wife and children behind, he finds urban, cosmopolitan Georgetown, with its wealthy and politically cynical Indian elite, an experience frequently at odds with the ardent simplicities of his teaching. In the tragi-comic absurdities of Devan's career, Dabydeen reveals powerfully the dangers to a religion's truths when it is made to serve the needs of ethnic assertion. But in becoming the Wizard Swami in charge of Mr Bhairam's prize racehorse Destiny, Devan not only reaches his lowest point, but also begins to discover truths of a much more tentative but enlightening kind. *The Wizard Swami* is a finely observed comedy of manners, but it is much more than that in its imaginative and poetic play with the symbols of Hinduism in a secular and cosmopolitan society.

Dark Swirl, 0-948833-20-3, £5.99

When a European naturalist arrives in a remote South American village, how are the villagers to respond to his promise to remove the monstrous massacouraman from the creek? Is he a saviour freeing them from its danger, or is he threatening to take away something which is uniquely theirs for display in an American or European zoo? Folk belief confronts rationalistic science in this poetic fable which sees events through both European and village eyes.

Set in the remote Canje region, the villagers in *Dark Swirl* feel that they have only the most vestigial remnants of their original Hindu world view. They have, indeed, absorbed much of the local mix of

Amerindian/African folk beliefs – in the existence of the legendary massacouraman, for instance. What they still have, though, is a residual Hindu view of the interconnectedness of all living things, though in their state of rootlessness this sometimes expresses itself in feelings of mutual hostility and unwarranted cruelty. Dreams are the interconnecting territory between the myth of the massacouraman and the innermost fantasies and intuitions of the villagers that relate to their fears concerning their loss of authenticity and their unbelonging. And it is in a dreamlike state induced by sickness, where he can no longer disentangle what is real from what is in his imagination, that the 'divided selves' of the European stranger begin speaking to him as: 'twin messengers with contrary tales.' In the process his whole structure of thought is profoundly altered.

Wilson Harris writes: 'Massacouraman is a formidable Guyanese folk legend... *Dark Swirl* seeks to plumb its pertinence to all factions, groups, races, insiders, outsiders. The novel seeks to evoke an inner region lying somewhere between the science of the stranger and the fantasies and visions of the village folk. Before they part company they appear to see through interchangeable eyes into the mysteries of a nature in a long state of eclipse...'

Berbice Crossing, 0-948833-69-6, £6.99

Cyril Dabydeen brings a poet's vision to these stories which span the crossing between the Caribbean and North America. They have a surface of gritty realism, but move inwards to explore the hidden dreams and latent capacities of his characters. Whether in the unsettling landscapes of rural Berbice in Guyana (with its ferocious crocodiles and even a spliff-toting Rasta), the wilderness of the Canadian North, or the urban melting pot of Toronto, Dabydeen's characters are memorably alert to what makes them feel either at home or alien in their various landscapes. Ranging from the extremely funny to the tragic, these stories are full of poetry, and sometimes terror. Cyril Dabydeen involves the reader creatively in a world of shifting grounds.

All available from www.peepaltreepress.com